THE NETWORK EFFECT

UNLOCKING SUCCESS THROUGH CONNECTIONS

Quantity sales and special discounts are available for bulk purchases by corporations, associations and others. For details, please reach out to CSI Publishing, listed above.

Orders by U.S. trade bookstores and wholesalers,

Email: ken@clientsi.com

The authors can be reached through Ken Walls.

Manufactured and printed in the United States of America, distributed globally by CSI Publishing - www.clientsi.com

Dallas, Texas

ISBN: 978-1-963986-19-8 Paperback

ISBN: 978-1-963986-18-1 Hardback

ISBN: 978-1-963986-20-4 eBook

Foreword

In every generation, the most successful people have shared one timeless truth: success is rarely achieved in isolation. Behind every breakthrough, every opportunity seized, and every dream realized, there is almost always a relationship—a connection that opened a door, offered guidance, or provided the courage to take the next step.

I know this from personal experience. Early in my career, when I was fresh out of college and trying to find my way in the business world, two remarkable women stepped into my life. They were both vendors at the time, but they became so much more than that. They each took me under their wing, teaching me not only about the mechanics of business but also about leadership, politics, and resilience. They helped me get around the right people and into the right rooms to help me learn and grow my network. What began as vendor relationships grew into mentorship and deep friendship. In turn, they became my trusted partners. As I grew from working on the ground floor of a specialty retailer to serving as vice president of an international company, I took them with me every step of the way. For more than fifteen years, we built success together.

That is the essence of the network effect. Relationships, when nurtured with care and authenticity, have the power to transform careers, businesses, and lives.

The Network Effect: Unlocking Success Through Connections is a powerful testament to this truth. Within these pages, nineteen accomplished professionals from diverse industries pull back the curtain on their journeys. They share not only the milestones of their careers, but the people and partnerships that made those milestones possible. Each story is a reminder that no matter our background or chosen field, the relationships we cultivate are often the most valuable assets we will ever build.

This book is not just a collection of stories—it's a roadmap. You'll find practical lessons about the art of authentic networking, the importance of showing up, and the compounding power of generosity. You'll see how leaders, entrepreneurs, and visionaries leaned on mentors, peers, and sometimes chance encounters to change the trajectory of their lives.

As you turn these pages, I encourage you to do more than just read. Reflect on your network. Consider who has shaped your journey and, just as importantly, who you can support along theirs. True networking is not about transactions—it is about transformation, both for ourselves and those around us.

May this book inspire you to expand your reach, strengthen your connections, and embrace the truth that success is best when shared.

— *Jill Walls*

Table of Contents

"You can have everything you want in life if you'll just help enough other people get what they want in life."

— Zig Ziglar

Glenn Morshower has appeared in more than 250 films and television shows, in a career spanning five decades. Audiences know Glenn best for his seven-year run as Agent Aaron Pierce, on the highly acclaimed FOX series 24, as General Morshower, in the Transformers films, as Wayne Lowry, on the Netflix original series Bloodline, and for the

past six years, he has had a running role as Marshall Winthrop, on the FOX series The Resident. Glenn also had a recurring role in the final season of the Netflix series Ozark.

Glenn has been on the big screen in The Little Things with Denzel Washington, Under the Stadium Lights with Laurence Fishburne, Bomb City, Transformers: The Last Knight, Aftermath, Curvature, and When the Bough Breaks. Some of his other film credits include Moneyball, After Earth, Parkland, X-Men: First Class, Men Who Stare at Goats, All the King's Men, Good Night & Good Luck, The Island, Hostage, Black Hawk Down, Pearl Harbor, Godzilla, Air Force One, The River Wild, Star Trek: Generations, FLUTTER, which he also produced, and The Doo Dah Man, which he won Best Actor for at the Monaco Film Festival.

Glenn founded and runs an online acting school called *The Extra Mile Working Actor's Workshop.* These live classes give working actors from all over the world the opportunity to study with Glenn and learn from each other. Everything from communication to script analysis to line delivery, timing, and preparing for auditions is part of the curriculum of Glenn's classes. His live role play and scene performances give each of the actors an opportunity to get direct feedback and coaching from a seasoned actor with more than 270 credits to his name in film, television, and video.

Glenn has been a professional speaker for thirty-eight years. His talks are on the subject of living an aligned life and having your dreams come true.

CHAPTER ONE

The Four Rooms of Expectancy

Moving from No to Yes in Life and Business

By Glenn Morshower

I am sitting here in Prosper, Texas, writing a chapter in a book with my buddy Ken Walls. My guess is that you are probably reading this same book right now. It's funny how things turn out that way.

This seems like a weird approach to authoring a book. In the past, I have always used a pen or a pencil. At what point did I forget that it's the year 2025? Today, I can actually sit and spill my thoughts into a microphone and allow the computer to do the writing for me. Ken showed me how easy it was, and BAM — I was hooked. Frankly, without Ken, I would be lost. I was technologically antiquated in every area of my life until I met him. He's a game changer. I would have named my children after him, but they were born 40 years before we met. Ken is an absolute legend. You get the point, moving on.

The Network Effect

When most people consider the idea of networking, they think in terms of hobnobbing around, shaking hands, meeting people, and perhaps even placing a few kisses on some butt cheeks. What folks need to learn is that those targeted cheeks tend to belong to successful people, who can smell a "bottom-smoocher" from a country mile away.

This style of networking is a colossal waste of time. Many believe in the old adage *"It's about who you know."* Nothing could be further from the truth. It's actually about *who knows you* — and who has you in the forefront of their thinking. This is a place all of us are capable of occupying when we learn to impact other human beings in a favorable way. It firmly places us in their consciousness.

I love the term my friend Garrett Gunderson uses: *relationship capital.* I've always believed that life rewards those who practice purity of intent. I've seen too many instances of this to believe otherwise. Life has an uncanny ability to support our dreams when our actions are rooted in the spirit of love and the heartfelt commitment to be of service.

I have spent the majority of my life both listening to and obeying internal mandates. I refer to them as whispers. Simply put, they are the Divine directives we are given to serve as the very rudder that determines the trajectory of our lives.

Sixteen years ago, one of those whispers paid me a visit in the shower. Strangely enough, it turns out this is a very common place to receive life instructions. I suspect it's something about the act of cleansing our bodies that enhances our ability to hear things from the invisible realm. In the old days, it would've been like cleaning the mud off the TV antenna on top of your roof — it results in receiving a clearer signal.

As a keynote speaker, I have surveyed audiences all over the country and found out that I am not alone in this discovery.

So, what was the whisper I heard? That silent voice (call it God, Life, Instinct, Intuition) revealed to me that there are **four**

distinctly different Rooms of Expectancy that all humans fall into.

Room 1: Impossibility

Theme word: *"no"*
This is the room of blame and victimization. When we reside in this room, we take zero responsibility for our role in day-to-day matters. Any suggestion that shows up in our minds is greeted by a veto — whether we are the one making the suggestion or not. The corresponding body posture is often that of crossed arms, suggesting resistance.

Room 2: Possibility

Theme word: *"maybe"*
This is known as the Room of Neutrality and the Birthplace of Listening. Residents of this room have upgraded their lives from a place of resistance to one of mindful consideration. Previously crossed arms tend to disappear here, replaced by openness.

Room 3: Probability

Theme word: *"likely"*
This room marks the beginning of elevated expectancy and is the Birthplace of Optimism. Residents of this room see all outcomes as favorable.

Room 4: Inevitability

Theme word: *"yes"*
The polar opposite of Room One. Residents of this room subscribe to the phrase *"things work out for me."* They are exciting people to be around — passion-filled, exuberant, and full of drive. There is a profound absence of WORRY here because it is replaced by the Spirit of Trust. Metaphorically speaking, people in this room tend to "jump out the window and grow wings on the way down."

Please ONLY see this as a metaphor and do not leap out of your nearest window. Chances are, the cement doesn't understand your optimism.

Navigating the Rooms

Relatability between residents of each room is a mere doorknob turn away:

- A Room 1 personality can engage with Room 2, but not Room 3.
- A Room 2 personality can engage with Room 1 or 3, but not Room 4.
- A Room 3 personality can engage with Room 2 or 4.

Does this make sense? If not, please discontinue reading now and skip to the next chapter — which, by the way, is on Nudity. Are you laughing? If not, then you probably shouldn't go out in public unsupervised.

The characteristics of each of the Four Rooms help us identify why certain relationships, when merged, seem to include inherent challenges. These difficulties come about due to a basic *incongruency of beliefs* held within each room. Theologians have taught us for years that *it is done unto us according to our beliefs.*

Therefore, each room experiences life through the lens of its own perception and believes itself to be true. Arguing to the contrary will prove futile. It is critical to understand the dynamics of each room to build the infrastructure of sustainable wellness.

Being aware of these Four Rooms helps us navigate the waters of relationship selection. The idea here is NOT to judge folks for the room they find themselves in — that would be as ridiculous as judging someone for their New York, Texas, or British accent.

Beliefs, like accents, are acquired through environmental absorption.

Conclusion

The reason I've opted to mention The Four Rooms of Expectancy is that networking, at its deepest level, refers to the ongoing relationship we have with our core beliefs. Metaphysical Law teaches us that we are incapable of experiencing anything that exceeds our existing belief system.

When we consciously choose to interact with a higher belief system, a long list of new things becomes available for us to experience. This approach to living increases our discipline and lays out the welcome mat for love, peace, and abundance.

Choose your room wisely. Your beliefs are your address — and life delivers to the address you give it. I wish you the very best in your journey!

After refusing to comply with Oregon's draconian COVID-19 lockdown in 2020, Lindsey was catapulted into the national spotlight. She

opened her salon against national mandates and became the iconic voice of freedom, being notoriously labeled "The Patriot Barbie" by the woke mob.

Her public defiance of government overreach was the bold act that opened the nation's eyes, as well as her own.

No stranger to battle, Lindsey publicly and authentically details both the grind and the glory of her life. Drawing on past experiences and real-world insights, Lindsey invites her audience into a journey that is both inspiring and encouraging. With vulnerability and candor, Graham openly details her colorful and powerful testimony, including her fall from grace and her fresh start after 2020. With strong faith and an unwavering conviction, Lindsey is now an American icon, blossoming from one life-altering moment in 2020.

Known for her viral activism and bold truth, Lindsey has become the fierce and unapologetic voice for Christians and women across America as one of the most inspiring speakers and influencers in our country.

Her candid and vibrant personality gives her fans and followers hope, backbone, and courage to unapologetically stand up for their rights, freedoms, and beliefs in the midst of a decaying culture.

Lindsey is a wife, a mom of three, a pro-life activist, a national keynote speaker, and a #1 Best Selling author, having published her memoir, *Targeted,* as well as an international children's faith-based book. She is the founder and President of Galatians Girl, a 501c3 non profit serving and supporting women.

A powerhouse entrepreneur, Lindsey is the founder and CEO of a conservative fashion brand, Pretty Little Patriot. She is also a partner and casting director with We The Studios streaming platform. Lindsey is also in the top 2% of a large network marketing company, and has branded her successful teams supporting over 250 women in business; My Freedom Cart and Tox Free Mom.

CHAPTER TWO
The Social Butterfly

Growing up, my mom was the life of every party. She was always wearing bright colors, attracting crowds, and socializing with everyone in the room. By the end of every event, everyone knew who she was and liked her. My dad called her a "social butterfly," flitting about the rooms, making friends and greeting everyone, leaving a beautiful impression on everyone she met. As I grew up, my dad began to say, "You are just like your mother, a little social butterfly." He was right.

Do you know what networking is? Networking is simply socializing, but with an agenda. Albeit a good agenda—building your connections and phone book with people of similar interests. Creating relationships with people you can serve or who may someday serve you. Generating currency in the form of connections, which will likely later benefit your movement, organization, or business for the better. But networking is really just socializing with a focus on business connections. So I guess, as a social butterfly, that qualifies me to be a networking expert.

My name is Lindsey Graham (not the senator from South Carolina). Online, I was labeled The Patriot Barbie in 2020 by radical cancel culture in Oregon, and it stuck. Since then, I have found my place in the conservative movement as an influencer, global keynote speaker, author, and eventually, once again, a successful entrepreneur. Since I can remember, I have embraced an entrepreneurial spirit. In 3rd grade, I began sneaking into my mom's craft room, staying up late to create custom bracelets with her supplies. I would then take them to school and sell them to my classmates at recess and at lunch. Imagine the profits I saw with zero overhead and a targeted demographic at my fingertips. The side gig became too popular, with my teacher calling home to tell my parents that my little business was becoming too distracting. That's how my mom discovered I was stealing her supplies to make a hustle. That was the first recollection I have of my nonstop, always evolving journey in entrepreneurship.

When it comes to business ideas and opportunities, my brain does not shut off. I am wired to create and build. Bracelet making at 8 years old was just the beginning. My entire life, I have embraced business and have not worked for anyone other than myself since I was 23 years old.

Why is networking one of the most important aspects of business? Because nothing we do is truly by ourselves. Your ego may believe that you are a one-man/woman show, but your connections, your network, your friends, and peers have played a vital role in your success, whether you prefer to give them credit or not. Who you know, how you know them, and how you use that information are major factors in your potential and past success. In fact, consider where many businesses and companies must find their customers and clients: either online, through social media marketing, promotions, and/or advertising. They typically are expected to pay for their business to get the attention it needs to function, grow, and profit. Or they could use the age-old trick—referrals and a complimentary program. (Read between the lines. A referral program is simply a way to pay people who are great at networking.) I am hoping that by the end of this chapter, my story will solidify this belief for you.

For the last five years, rebuilding the empire that was lost, I have recognized the incomprehensible benefits of my relationships and businesses based on one simple factor: networking. After being canceled in Oregon, I lost six businesses and was forced to move, with no future, no career, no financial security, and no endeavors on the horizon. The only way I could dream of building a new life would be to make connections in the area that I moved to.

When I had a deep conversation with God about the path my life was taking, I was shocked to learn that I was not immediately meant to go back to doing what I had done very successfully for 15 years. In Oregon, I was an established salon owner and hair stylist, boasting 25 chairs in my 5,000-square-foot salon, serving clients three days a week, and a successful retail and e-commerce hair extension company, offering sales in my salon and to other stylists, as well as clients. I was very talented and applied entrepreneurialism to every aspect of my business until my salon expanded to its fullest capacity. Upon losing this business to cancel culture and being forced to close, it was safe to assume that upon moving to a new state, I would simply rebuild, as devastating as it felt.

I was wrong. God called me to write my first book, *Targeted*, and it was the shock of my life. I had never published anything before and was unsure what I was supposed to write about that would be of any interest. Turns out, while writing, God was revealing His plan for my life and revealing to me that He had prepared me for a very different path that I was unaware of. After writing *Targeted*, which turned out to be my testimony, I gave my life completely to God, told Him I trusted Him, and then waited for Him to lead me.

Here is where He did. Nowhere dramatic, at first. Seemingly unimportant events with strangers. But I was obedient, and God knew that if He would put me in rooms with certain people, I would leave connected to them, being the "little social butterfly" that I am. I prayed each day for God to open the doors He wanted me to go through, and He did. I began accepting invitations to political events as a guest and made sure to meet as many people as I could in the room. I always left the events with 5–10 new phone numbers in my phone. I didn't know why I needed their contact info or what role they would play in my life, but I made connections, and I developed relationships.

When I tell you that one person would connect me to someone else, who would connect me to someone else, I don't know how to emphasize enough that every single room I have been in the last five years came from a completely unexpected connection years earlier—or a connection of a connection. You get the point. Reminding you again that I personally had no agenda in connecting and building relationships with these people, I simply built a phone book knowing that someday, these connections may be useful, or that I may be useful to them. Within five years, I had met people who had opened door after door, leading me into opportunities I never would have dreamed of.

By 2024, these relationships and connections had led to some of the most incredible opportunities I could dream of. At Mar-A-Lago, I was called out from the crowd by President Donald Trump. I was asked to come forward, speak with him, and shake his hand. The only reason this happened was because of a connection I accepted for a completely different reason two years earlier. I have filmed conversations with Tucker Carlson in his green room, having been invited by a connection that I had made a year earlier at a women's event. Friends, when I am meeting these people, I have no idea what I have to offer them, or they me. I am not looking at them like a piece of meat and what I can get from them, or who they know. I am simply recognizing that we are like-minded, we should stay in touch, and someday there may come an opportunity to do great things together. If that is your motive behind building a network, you cannot go wrong. The person who invited me to Mar-A-Lago was not a person I would have expected to open those kinds of doors to me for years down the road. You never know what your relationships are going to lead to. The woman who invited me to meet Tucker Carlson is a pro-gun Texas mom, who I was simply enjoying a friendship with. I would have never imagined she would lead to such an incredible opportunity.

You make a connection not to use and abuse them. Not to manipulate or take advantage of them. You make the connection because the business world operates on who knows the right person at the right time for the job and who can connect you. When your phone book has hundreds and hundreds of people, you are more likely to know someone that can help. You become the person everyone calls when they "need a guy," which ironically ends up multiplying your contacts as well. What a fabulous reputation to have! You are the person people know and trust for suggesting contacts and connections. You don't ask for anything in return or make radical demands. You become a reputable connector with good intentions, and that reputation alone will expand your network.

Now, let's reverse the process. When you need the right person for the job, you have it at your fingertips. You don't have to go scrounging like a stray dog in the dumpster, looking for someone who wants to work with you and praying they are a good fit. You either have that person on your phone already, or you know someone that knows someone. And nothing feels better than people recognizing you as the person who "knows someone." You become an asset to everyone you meet. You become the person everyone wants to meet, because you know all the right people. You help your fellow entrepreneur when they need contacts, and your reputation in the industry (any industry) is that you are the person to call.

Let me give you one great example of the importance of connections, whether you know at the time what value they bring. I was contacted by a local friend in my community about a possible connection he wanted to make. A friend of his had created a water filtration system that he thought I and my audience online would appreciate. I said yes. I almost always say yes. It's why I am where I am. I say yes 100 times more than I say no. Nelson had a great water system; I use it to this day. But Nelson and I have gone on to do so many business transactions together. I connected him to my network, and he has blessed my contacts and worked with them. Nelson has connected me to some amazing people and opened up his network to me. A random stranger with a water filtration system has turned into one of the greatest assets in my phone book.

Nelson was sponsoring an event at Trump International Golf Club in Palm Beach. He reached out to tell me about it, assuming my fashion brand Pretty Little Patriot might want to sponsor; we did. But when the hosts discovered I was a keynote speaker, I was also invited to speak. This led to an entire weekend of invitations to a variety of events at Mar-A-Lago, including Nelson inviting me to a breakfast the next day. At that breakfast, President Donald Trump came in to say hello, liked the red bow I was wearing, and called me up to meet me. Because I had spoken the day before, the crowd cheered, "It's the Patriot Barbie," as I walked up to meet Trump. The President of the United States of America knows who I am and has shaken my hand. Why? Because I took a call from a water filtration guy three years prior for no reason. I had no idea or plans for going into a conversation with Nelson. No agenda or motive. I was simply willing to accept a connection. That connection led to my meeting the President. Meeting Trump was the highlight, but you better believe that I got 10 more phone numbers in that room that day also, to add to my network.

I could give another example about my friend Ken Walls here, the author of this book you hold in your hands. I was a guest on his podcast in 2024. After the show, we stayed online and began discussing our ventures, who we know, how we can help each other. Ending the call, we both knew that we would do great things together when the time was right. When I wrote my children's book *Alphabet Prayers for Toddlers* and needed a publisher, guess who I called? The man that was already in my phone book that I had built a relationship with. It was a great decision—Ken launched my book to be an Amazon bestseller, and it is published in the Library of Congress. I think it's safe to say that as you read this, Ken and I are still working together, presenting each other with opportunities. When Ken needs a connection, he may call me first. When my connections need someone of his expertise, I am going to send them to him. No contract, no verbal commitment. Just networking doing what it does best: providing entrepreneurs their greatest asset—connections.

I have not gone to college. I have no degree. I have never taken business classes. In high school, I would not have been voted "most likely to succeed." It doesn't take training or years of school to network. It doesn't take a degree to socialize. What it takes is a desire to serve others, to have connections, and use them to further your friendships, relationships, and partnerships. A rising tide lifts all ships. When you build a network that holds value, you build your own personal value in the business world. When you use that value to serve others, bless others, and aid those you've brought into your network, you create success around you. I was never set on a path to become an entrepreneur, and sometimes I am shocked by the doors that have opened because of my obedience and networking.

Here is my advice: say yes. Go to every event that you can. Speak to everyone you can. Connect with everyone you can. Please don't look for the wealthiest person in the room, or the most famous person in the room. Don't look for an agenda. You are not looking for anyone who can offer you something. You are looking to create relationships that have value, either now or down the road. You are looking for the greatest asset you can possibly own in business: a thick and valuable phone book.

My journey is a great example of how networking can explode your ventures. I went from losing six businesses to an empire even greater and more valuable than before. I have now written two books, I am a global keynote speaker, I own an e-commerce and storefront clothing boutique called Pretty Little Patriot, and I am in the top 2% of a 40-billion-dollar company in direct sales. I have never had a sales job in my life. I had never done network marketing. But with my connections and the reputation I have built in being trustworthy, I have built a business that thrives on residual income and will provide a legacy for my children the rest of our lives. As an entrepreneur, my greatest source of income is network marketing. Friends, the proof is in the pudding. Multi-level marketing is based on who you know and who trusts you. I am more successful in this endeavor than in anything else I do, and the entire model is based on networking. In fact, my organization has grown so large so quickly that we have had to brand out segments of our team into promotional talking points just to streamline overwhelming interest in our team. Because of networking, I also now have a vast array of patriotic partnerships and multiple ambassador and brand deals. All the businesses I am now running are successful because of the people I have met and connected with in the last four years.

For so many, maybe even someone reading this looking for their next endeavor, the American dream of being an independent, self-made, even wealthy business owner seems a distant and far-fetched fantasy. To work for yourself and answer to no one. To set your own hours and make your own goals. To set your goals and then exceed them, while continuing to dream bigger and bigger at every milestone. That is the American dream for so many entrepreneurial-minded people. And very few have what it takes to discipline themselves to get here.

In the same breath, we curse what we think would have been necessary to achieve these dreams. Growing up wealthy, having a secure family, a great childhood, a good education, opportunities... wait. Stop there. Opportunities. No matter where you grew up, how you were raised, or what your childhood was like, you have been given the same gift as everyone else in life: opportunities. They may not be grandiose or spectacular—in fact, you may not even see them while you're facing them. But an opportunity is in every room, at every corner, on every phone call, and in everyone you meet. Why? Because an opportunity to grow your connections is a chance to put currency in your pocket that perhaps the other people in the room didn't consider. I think by now you understand what I mean by currency. The single greatest currency in business is not your customer. It's not your client. It's not your credit. The greatest asset consumed by anyone in any business—what makes you more valuable than the person who is more educated, professional, or experienced—is your network of connections.

Don't you wonder why you see influential, successful entrepreneurs having "mixers" and "networking events" all the time? Before this chapter, you may have asked yourself, "What's the point? You can't all be doing business together all the time. You can't support every payment processor you meet.

You can't bank with every banker. You can't publish your book with every publisher." Everyone is a realtor, or a podcaster, or a clothing designer, or a _____ (fill in the job that it seems everyone has). The reason that mixers and networking events are so resourceful is that the people you meet may not need your business now, but they may need it later. Or they may have a friend that needs it now, or, heck, they may have a friend that needs it later. When that time comes, you want YOUR number to be on their phone. And just as important, your career may change, and you may need to access someone for reasons you never anticipated. Your connections could help you on the next business venture you take or the next opportunity that's presented to you. Perhaps someone in your phone book will be the person to present you with a new opportunity.

This chapter is not to tell you how to network. Networking needs to be genuine, authentic, and easy. You cannot force real relationships, and you cannot always put yourself in the rooms you want to be in. This chapter is to reinforce your belief in networking and what it brings to your business, life, platforms, or organizations. This chapter is to encourage you to find opportunities to surround yourself with people who think like you do and have a desire to curate connections for the greater good of everyone they connect with. This chapter is to remind you that if you want to do great things in greater measure, you are not doing it successfully if you are doing it alone. You need a network that you have established genuine working relationships with to come alongside you and generate even more connections and opportunities for you, as you do for them.

Your greatest skill, your greatest asset, your greatest value is in networking. If you want to build a business, build a phone book; if you want to build an empire, build connections; if you want to build a legacy, build relationships.

"You are the average of the five people you spend the most time with."

– Jim Rohn

Sharla J. Frost is a nationally recognized trial attorney, bestselling author, and sought-after speaker with more than three decades of

legal experience. She began her career in litigation and went on to found and manage a successful boutique law firm, later serving in leadership roles at regional and national firms. Known for her skill in high-stakes trials, her strategic business development expertise, and her ability to mentor other lawyers, Sharla has built a reputation as both a formidable advocate and a generous leader in the legal profession.

Over the course of her career, Sharla has represented clients across the United States in complex, high-profile cases, earning the respect of colleagues, adversaries, and clients alike. She is celebrated not only for her command in the courtroom but also for her innovative approach to building client relationships and growing a sustainable law practice.

In addition to her legal work, Sharla is a prolific author. Her books include the original *Power at the Table: The Woman Lawyer's Guide to Gaining Clients and Control* and its expanded edition, *Power at the Table²: The Lawyer's Guide to Gaining Clients and Control*. She is also the author of the *Frogville* children's series and a contributing author to several bestselling anthologies on entrepreneurship, leadership, and personal success.

A frequent keynote speaker and trainer, Sharla has presented to bar associations, legal conferences, and business organizations nationwide. Her engaging style blends candid storytelling with actionable strategies, empowering lawyers at every stage of their careers to define their vision, attract their ideal clients, and take control of their professional destinies.

When she's not in the courtroom or on stage, Sharla remains committed to mentoring the next generation of lawyers, advocating for professional excellence, and contributing to the communities she serves. Her work continues to inspire attorneys to not just earn a seat in the room, but to claim their power at the table.

CHAPTER THREE

More Than a Business Card: The Power of Real Connection

In the end, we'll remember the connections that carried us, the kindnesses we shared, and the laughter that filled the in-between spaces. Let that be the work worth doing.

In the high-stakes world of business and law, success is often measured in billable hours, case outcomes, and bottom-line figures. But what if the true marker of a meaningful career lies not in the fluorescent-lit offices or the polished patter of boardroom presentations, but in the laughter shared over lunch, the understanding glance across a courtroom, or the simple grace of being present when presence matters most?

Personal connections and friendships are not just embellishments; they are the foundation on which we build both careers and lives. Relationships are not distractions from the work—they are the work. They transform a job into a calling, and colleagues into cherished friends. We each come to our business development journey by a different path. However, we share the ultimate goals: the freedom and flexibility that comes from having your own clientele. That clientele becomes part of your personal framework of connections and family.

We seek not just professional success, but professional belonging. We want clients who trust us, colleagues who respect us, and a network that nourishes us. In the end, we want to be able to pick up the phone, call someone we trust, and know the conversation won't require pretense. We want to work with people we like. That desire is not a weakness; it is the human condition at work. When we lean into it, we don't dilute our professional edge—we sharpen it with real connection.

The Emotional Architecture of Business

Life has an emotional architecture—a framework composed of those who lift us, listen to us, and walk alongside us. That scaffolding, when carefully and lovingly constructed, not only catches us when we stumble but also gives us the confidence to reach higher.

Think back. How many of your pivotal career breaks came from job postings or formal applications? And compare that to how many were born out of conversations, introductions, shared experiences? The old adage says that it isn't what you know, it is who you know that counts, but that is only partly true. In this modern environment, who knows you is as important - if not more important - than who you know. But whether the person is someone you know or someone who simply knows you, those connections—direct or indirect—give you the crucial building blocks of your career and your life.

A warm introduction, a well-timed recommendation, a word of encouragement from someone you admire—these are the gifts that open doors. They cost nothing and mean everything. But you must cultivate connections before you need them. Waiting until you need something before you decide to tend to your network is like trying to grow a garden during a drought. Connections, like a good harvest, take patience, water, and light. The time commitment is real, yet the outcome more than justifies it.

My own legal career took shape in large part because of the people who believed in me, recommended me, and walked beside me through trial after trial. Professional relationships became friendships. And those friendships became the lights that guide me. When my boss came to me and asked me to start a law firm with him and become his business partner, it was his faith in my ability to succeed that created the opportunity. When I ran that idea past my father's 80-something-year-old lawyer friend, he gave me the advice and confidence I needed to take that chance. When I decided to pivot from trial work to whatever was going to come next, it was a fellow graduate from my old high school who pointed me in the direction of my next venture.

Each of those connections helped advance my life.

We learn the principles of law or commerce in school. But we learn connection through living. And like any learned discipline, friendship and human interaction demand intention, care, and a touch of courage. You have to seek out advice, like-minded contacts, and trusted counselors. People provide the support and structure you need. Books and internet resources cannot replicate that human touch—even if they can clone their voices!

Solace in Shared History

A few years ago, I attended a memorial service for an old friend—one of those gatherings where memories and emotions weave into something sacred. The evening felt more like an Irish wake than a somber event. There was laughter. There were tears. And yes, there was champagne—cheap, fizzy, and perfect. The kind we had toasted with years earlier in our law school days at the famed Cheap Champagne party in Waco, Texas, where the participants were required to each bring a bottle, and no bottle could cost more than $10, since we were poor law students. The alcohol was more expensive now that we were all working adults, but the connections shared were even more priceless.

That memorial evening wasn't just a memory; it was a mirror. In sharing stories of our friend Mark, we reconnected with who we were and who we had become. That tapestry of friendship was richer than any resume. Making connections matters. Keeping them matters more. Staying in touch over the years takes effort. That electronic calendar can track birthdays, but it can't buy and send the birthday card. You need to do that. The endless rerun of a favorite, shared movie can make you laugh, but the television can't generate the phone call to recount old times with your old college roommate. You have to type in those numbers.

True solace comes from being seen, known, and remembered. That only happens when we live authentically and make space for others to do the same. Whether it's at a memorial or a garden party, it's those connections that matter most. Tending to your friendships deserves the same focus that you pay to your business tasks. Use that electronic calendar to carve out time for the personal connections in the same way that you track your business events. Stay in touch to stay connected.

Friendship as Strategic Advantage

There is a stark difference between networking and friendship. The former often feels like collecting names; the latter, like collecting stories. Business cards can get lost in drawers. But a shared moment? A moment lasts. There is a reason that people attend class reunions and get-togethers: the quality and quantity of shared moments create bonds that refresh the soul.

Genuine friendships in business confer an advantage that algorithms can't quantify. The camaraderie that comes from shared experience cannot be bought or faked. Boot camp for the military is as much about creating a glue of shared experience as it is about teaching skills. Lifelong friendships grow out of joint survival. Hours spent together on a shared project forge shared memories. I vividly remember the hours spent frantically trying to understand the language of the law during my first weeks of law school. Sharing that experience with other liberal arts graduates like me created bonds that exist to this day. They became more than classmates; they became my friends. And they have stayed my friends.

In a similar fashion, clients and colleagues became friends through time shared in often difficult situations. Hours spent fashioning and revising arguments in the middle of the night gave way to shared exuberance (or depression) at the outcome. Through the commonality of experience, those work strangers became friends, as well. They provide the professional glue that holds a career together.

I have a treasured photograph of me with a client at the St. Patrick's Day parade in New York City. We had been frantically preparing for a trial when one of the trial team summarily turned off the lights and insisted that all of us go down the street and watch the parade. The mental break helped decrease the stress. The shared experience on the crowded street made for a lasting connection. Experience became memory. Connections became permanent. Client became friend.

These are the moments that define your trajectory—not because they make you more popular or polished, but because they remind you that you are part of something larger than yourself. And that knowledge is power.

Real friends advocate for your promotion. They check in when the world gets heavy. They cheer the loudest when you succeed and offer solace when you don't. And perhaps most importantly, they keep you grounded. I still vividly remember the call from a friend after I had lost a challenging trial. I was devastated. I wasn't sure I ever wanted to go through that process again. He called to tell me that if I would just lose a few more tens of millions of dollars, he would hire me. He explained that only great lawyers had the chance to lose again, and that he felt certain I would have that chance. He not only cheered me up, he gave me hope. And it turned out he was right. I had the chance to fight another day in another courtroom. He trusted me.

Influence does not stem from perfection. It grows from trust. And trust is cultivated through consistency, empathy, and shared experience. Build that, and doors open. My friend gave me both the uplift and the emotional support I needed. His influence resonated well beyond the phone call. Be the person who makes the phone call for the person who needs it. The universe will return the favor when you are the one who needs that support.

The Illusion of Independence

Many of us were raised on the myth of rugged individualism—especially in law, where self-reliance is a badge of honor. The courtroom image of the lone warrior—sharp, relentless, autonomous—is baked into our professional culture. But the truth is: no one argues a case, builds a business, or authors a legacy alone.

Behind every successful moment is an invisible thread of support—mentors, partners, friends, rivals—all contributing to our growth. Even the fiercest solo practitioner draws from a constellation of experience, encouragement, and memory. I have taken many stages and stood in many courtrooms, but I have never truly stood alone. I carry with me the voices, challenges, and kindnesses of many. That quiet chorus is always there.

To acknowledge our interdependence is not to show weakness—it is to embrace wisdom. Community doesn't diminish our strength; it multiplies it. Every strong person I know has someone they call when they feel weak. Every leader has someone they ask for help when they face the unknown. We should not fear these confessions of humanity—we should honor them.

So much of the stress professionals feel—particularly women in law and leadership roles—stems from the false belief that asking for help equates to failure. Let me say clearly: there is no valor in unnecessary isolation. Asking for support, advice, or just a listening ear is not failure; it is stewardship of your strength. And the people who help you? They aren't doing you a favor—they're building a connection. And when you return the favor, you're doing the same.

Reclaiming Connection in a Disconnected Age

We live in a time of performative engagement, rather than personal connections. Social media offers dopamine and detachment in equal measure. We "like" posts instead of talking, send emojis instead of expressing empathy, and mistake performance for presence. And yet, beneath all the scrolling and posting, the need for real connection pulses stronger than ever.

Authentic connection requires more than visibility. It requires vulnerability. It's showing up—not just physically, but emotionally. It's checking in with an old friend, not because you need something, but because you miss the sound of their voice. It's sending a note of encouragement to a former client just because you remember how nervous they were that day in court. It's recognizing that our humanity is our most enduring brand.

Try it. Reach out to someone you have not talked to in a while. Write a note. Send a message. Invite them to something just because you want their company. Or better yet, show up with a bottle of champagne (cheap or not) and say, "Let's talk."

The return on this kind of outreach is hard to quantify, but impossible to overstate. People remember how you made them feel. They remember who stayed in touch, who called when they didn't have to, who showed up with a cookie and stayed to talk about nothing in particular. These are the roots of trust. And trust is the root of opportunity. Clients hire those people they know, like, and trust. You want to be one of those people, both in your personal and professional roles.

Beyond the Resume

Beneath every title and accolade hides a person. And it is that person—that unfiltered, authentic self—who others want to connect with. Everyone craves the comfort of realness. Authenticity is not just the new catch phrase; it is the reality that people seek.

Some of my most enduring professional relationships began in the least formal places: a hot dog stand on a Manhattan Street after a hearing, a hallway bench in a Los Angeles courthouse, a fundraising gala, a grocery store line, an Uber ride with an interesting driver. Connection doesn't care where you are; it cares that you're open. As many of my business referrals have come from former adversaries as from colleagues.

When we invite others to know the person we are, not just the position we hold, we create friendships that outlast job changes and career pivots. I'm still friends with my seatmate from first grade. He and I have been friends through job changes, life changes, and world changes. That connection mattered when it started and continues to matter now that we are later in life. My most recent work assignment came from a recommendation of a former opposing counsel with whom I developed a working relationship after hours of negotiations and serious arm-twisting. He told me that I was the only one he could think of whom he would trust to tell him the truth about the project for which he proposed my involvement. (He did not, however, promise to follow my advice.) He came to know my personality, rather than my work title. That connection mattered, too.

Your connections have the same kind of value. And your story—the one you live every day—is your most valuable business card.

Intentional Circles

You do not need to know everyone. You just need to know your people. And those people—your true circle—should be chosen with care. Build your circle like you'd plant a garden: intentionally, seasonally, with the full awareness that some connections will thrive quickly, while others may take years to bloom.

Cultivate relationships with people who challenge you to grow, who will be honest even when it stings, and who make space for your voice. Choose collaborators who see you not just for what you do, but for who you are. Surround yourself with those who believe in your dreams, and who will gently nudge you forward when you doubt yourself. Learn to let go of the ones who do not nurture you. Find the people who nurture you and who you can nurture in return. Those are the relationships that make life fuller and more rewarding.

Make room for mentors who have walked the road ahead of you, and peers who walk beside you now. Include in your circle those who make you laugh, those who inspire you to think differently, and those who will sit with you quietly when you need comfort more than counsel. Mentor others. Make space in your life for the next generation—people you can encourage and pour into, because wisdom shared is wisdom sustained. Others supported you. Be sure you repay the universe by doing the same for those who need your insight and support.

And remember to be *that* person for others. Bring the soup. Lend the ear. Share the joy. Make the referral. Give the recommendation. Open the bottle, whether it is champagne or a cold Dr. Pepper. There is no act too small to plant a seed of friendship and life connection.

Technology and the Texture of Connection

We live in an era of extraordinary communication tools, and yet loneliness and isolation are quietly rising. It's a paradox of our times: we are always reachable yet rarely reached. Technology, with all its magic, has altered the way we connect—but not always for the better.

A quick tap on a screen can replace a conversation. A reaction emoji can stand in for a real response. We substitute presence with availability, but one is not the same as the other. Face-to-face moments, where tone, pause, posture, and presence all shape the exchange, are harder to come by—and more valuable than ever.

We've grown accustomed to a kind of digital shorthand for engagement. But that shortcut often erases the subtlety and soul of genuine relationships. Texts can be efficient, but they rarely build intimacy. Video calls can bridge geography, but they're not a substitute for sitting across the table from someone and reading the quiet things they aren't saying aloud. Nothing replaces the evolutionary significance of looking deeply into the eyes of the person across the table from you. The pixels that represent those eyes on the computer screen don't convey the same evidence of truth or falsity.

Technology can be a wonderful bridge. But we must be careful not to let it become a barrier. Use it to open the door—not to close it. Let it serve as a starting point, not the destination.

Ask yourself: Am I using this tool to deepen my relationship, or just to check a box? Am I relying on efficiency where empathy is needed? Am I trading connection for convenience? Convenience sometimes plays a role, but it is not a substitute for the human touch.

The most meaningful relationships are not built through convenience. They are built through intention. A handwritten note still carries weight. A spontaneous phone call can heal more than any perfectly crafted email. A coffee meeting can restore what dozens of messages could never reach.

Connection in the age of technology is possible—but only if we choose it. Be the person who makes time. Who listens. Who sees. Who shows up.

The Legacy We Leave

When all is said and done, none of us will be remembered for the titles we held or the trophies that gathered dust on our shelves. We will be remembered for how we made people feel. For the way we listened. For the way we loved.

That's the reason I write children's books. I want to be remembered for making people think and smile. You don't have to go to that same extreme to leave a legacy, but you should find a way to be the person who makes other people's lives better. You can do that by improving their day, whether through an uplifting card or by solving their most pressing problem with grace and integrity.

Legacy is not about size; it's about substance. It's not about wealth; it's about warmth. And the beautiful thing about warmth is that it expands. Each kind gesture, each shared laugh, each moment of honest connection becomes a ripple. One conversation today becomes a fond memory tomorrow— and possibly a life-changing moment for someone else in the future.

When it's my turn to be toasted at the proverbial Irish Wake, I hope the champagne flutes are clinking—whether they hold bubbly or Diet Dr. Pepper. I hope the room echoes with laughter. I hope the stories are full of life and mischief and a few spectacular wardrobe malfunctions. That's the legacy I want: not one of perfection, but one of presence.

Because in the long run, it's the relationships we've nurtured that endure. Not the deals. Not the deadlines. But the people. The ones who knew us, the ones who trusted us, the ones who remembered us.

And yes, let's have some champagne. Every event deserves a little sparkle.

"Alone, we can do so little; together, we can do so much."

– Helen Keller

James Beaudoin is an entrepreneur, family man, and community leader from Avon, Connecticut, who believes deeply in the transformative power of authentic networking. Though he built his career in

the transportation and lawn care industries, his true passion lies in helping people grow through meaningful connections. An introvert by nature, James discovered that networking isn't about collecting business cards or social media contacts—it's about listening deeply, asking thoughtful questions, and giving without expectation.

His journey has taken him from striking up everyday conversations in coffee shops to knocking on thousands of doors while campaigning for local office, and from building friendships in his hometown to joining national mastermind groups like the Arete Syndicate, founded by Andy Frisella and Ed Mylett. Along the way, he has learned that success is never a solo journey—it is built in community. Guided by his belief that *"everyone you meet can teach you something,"* James continues to cultivate connections that fuel both professional success and personal fulfillment, while cherishing his most important role as husband and dad, where family remains the heart of his success.

CHAPTER 4

The Power of Networking: Cultivating Connections for Success

by James Beaudoin, Avon, CT

"Everyone you meet can teach you something."

The first time I truly understood the power of networking wasn't in a conference room or at some industry mixer. It was when I realized that if one person can achieve something, so can another. If they've done it, that means it's possible. The only difference between them and you is knowledge, experience, and sometimes the right introductions.

Networking, for me, became the simple but profound recognition that you can learn how to improve in every way possible from people who have already done the things you want to do. Learn about them. Watch how they accomplished their goals. And then, if you're willing to put yourself out there, you can follow in their footsteps while still making the path your own.

From Introvert to Initiator

I'll be honest: I'm an introvert by nature. For a long time, I thought that meant I was at a disadvantage in the networking game. You know the type — the natural extroverts who seem to float effortlessly through a room, shaking hands, laughing loudly, collecting admirers like candy. That wasn't me.

But here's the truth: being an introvert is not a limitation. It's a skill set. Introverts tend to listen more, process before speaking, and notice details others miss. Those qualities are gold in building authentic relationships.

The shift for me came when I realized I had to get comfortable being uncomfortable. That meant ignoring the voice in my head that said, "Don't bother that person" or "Wait for them to come to you" — and doing the exact opposite.

I started practicing in the most ordinary settings. Standing in line at the coffee shop, I'd ask the person next to me what pastry pairs best with their drink because "I'd love to give it a try." In the grocery store, I'd compliment someone's shoes and ask where they found them because "I've been looking for some like those." On a plane, I'd turn to the person beside me and ask where they were from and what they liked to do outside of work.

Not everyone responded warmly, and that's fine. The goal wasn't to make instant best friends — it was to make talking to strangers feel natural. Over time, those little conversations became a muscle I could flex at will.

"Be comfortable being uncomfortable — it's where the growth happens."

The Numbers Game That Didn't Work

When I first started thinking seriously about networking, I got it completely wrong. I thought the point was to meet as many people as possible, shake their hands, hand out my business card, or add them to my social media "friends" list. My goal was to rack up numbers — to get to some magic total of contacts that would mean I'd finally "made it."

It turns out people don't respond to that at all.

The truth is that collecting business cards isn't networking. Having a thousand LinkedIn connections you've never spoken to isn't networking. What matters isn't the number — it's the depth.

The secret is in listening. Real listening. Genuine curiosity. The kind that makes someone feel heard and seen. That's not something you can fake, and it's not something you can rush.

It's a skill. And like any skill, it can be practiced. The more you practice being curious, the better you become.

"It's better for 1,000 people to know YOU than for you to know 1,000 people."

A Chance Meeting That Stuck

In 2019, I attended a business conference in Miami. That's where I met Jacob Godar, who happens to be a co-author of this very book. He's in the same industry as I am, but in a completely different part of the country. He runs his business in Florida, and I run mine in Connecticut.

At the time, I had no idea that a casual conversation at that event would turn into one of the most important professional friendships in my life. Jacob and I still talk at least once a month. We text all the time. And despite being hundreds of miles apart, we've found that many of our challenges are the same.

When I hit a problem in my business, I know I can reach out to him. He might see things from an angle I've missed, and one insight can save me weeks of stress. I try to do the same for him.

That's what networking is at its best: two people helping each other, learning from each other, holding each other accountable, and celebrating wins together.

Jacob and I didn't meet because I was running around trying to collect contacts. We met because I showed up, stayed open, and let a relationship develop.

Campaigning for Connection

A few years ago, I got it in my head that I might want to run for local office, but I had no idea where to begin. The world of politics felt like a locked room with no visible door.

Then I remembered something: one of my lawn care clients was on our local town council. I gave her a call, and we had a great conversation. She introduced me to other members of the local party, and before I knew it, I was out campaigning with them.

Within six months, I went from "I don't know where to start" to knocking on over a thousand doors in my community, attending and hosting fundraisers, sign-waving at busy intersections, and shaking so many hands on Election Day. But here's what surprised me most: I wasn't just campaigning. I was making friends.

Those conversations at front doors weren't just about issues or votes. They were about kids, jobs, favorite restaurants, and hometown stories. By the end of that campaign, I knew more about my neighbors — and they knew more about me — than I ever thought possible.

Networking doesn't always look like "business." Sometimes it looks like knocking on doors until your knuckles hurt, only to walk away with friendships that last far beyond the campaign.

Give Without Expecting

One of the most powerful lessons I've learned about networking is that the real magic happens when you stop trying to get something out of it.

Take the story of one of my construction-industry connections. One day, he asked me how to make his lawn look better. I own a lawn fertilization company, so I shared some advice. I wasn't trying to sell him anything. I wasn't thinking "lead generation." I was just trying to help.

That conversation turned into my team taking care of 26 lawns in his housing community, because he just so happened to also be the President of it. He appreciated the sincerity. He appreciated that I wasn't trying to "close" him. And because I wasn't trying to get something, he chose to give me a lot of business.

That's reciprocity in action. When you give freely, people remember it.

"Give first. Help first. The rewards will come later, often in ways you never expect."

The Power of Mastermind

Networking isn't only about one-to-one relationships. Sometimes it's about joining a room where everyone is committed to growing together.

For me, that place has been the Arete Syndicate — a business entrepreneurship group founded by Andy Frisella and Ed Mylett. Arete is a group of high-performing entrepreneurs who believe in using business as a force for good. Andy often says, *"It's not one person or one government that will change the world — it's entrepreneurs."*

But Arete is about more than just business. It's about excellence. It's about surrounding yourself with people who are building not just companies but lives that make the world a better place, and we could all use more of that!

At "Arete Syndicate Live" in St. Louis in 2019, I met more than 20 entrepreneurs from all over the country in a single weekend. None of us came to sell. We came to share, to learn, and to challenge each other to level up. These were not people who talked about "someday." They were people who made things happen, who held each other accountable to the highest standards. Conversations flowed easily but with purpose — one minute we were sharing strategies for scaling a business, the next we were challenging each other to step up in our health, relationships, or community involvement.

I left that weekend not just with new contacts but with new friends, new ideas, and a deeper commitment to building something meaningful. That's the power of putting yourself in the right room.

When Business Becomes Friendship

Not every connection has to stay "professional." Some of the best ones evolve into something more.

I once reached out to an insurance agent I knew through Arete — let's call him "Q" — because I needed some advice. He gave me his time and insight freely, without trying to pitch me on his services. Eventually, I did become his client, but by then, the business part felt secondary.

Over months of working through policies and renewals, we shared stories about our families and lives. We became friends. Real friends. Q wasn't just looking out for my business needs; he was looking out for me as a person.

That's when I realized something: the strongest networks are built on trust, generosity, and genuine care. The business flows naturally from there, but it's not the centerpiece. The relationship is.

The Wisdom of Literature

While human connections form the heartbeat of networking, books are the lungs — breathing in knowledge and exhaling perspective. Reading equips you to connect on a deeper level because it sharpens your empathy, expands your vocabulary, and gives you new ways to engage.

One of my favorite books is "Unreasonable Hospitality" by Will Guidara. It's not about networking directly, but it is about relationships. Guidara teaches that business isn't just about transactions, it's about experiences. It's about making people feel seen, valued, and cared for. Imagine taking that mindset into your networking: treating every person not as a potential client or colleague, but as a guest deserving of your full attention and generosity. That's what creates lasting impact.

Classics like Dale Carnegie's "How to Win Friends and Influence People" or Stephen Covey's "7 Habits of Highly Effective People" reinforce the same lesson. Success is less about charisma and more about caring. When you read books like these, you're not just filling your mind — you're stocking your toolkit for connection.

Choosing the Right Circle

The people you spend the most time with shape you in ways you can't always see. If your circle is small-minded, negative, or complacent, it will quietly pull you down. But if your circle is ambitious, generous, and creative, it will pull you up.

Mentors and mentees are part of that circle. Sometimes you'll be the one giving wisdom, sometimes you'll be receiving it. Don't underestimate reverse mentoring either — younger or less experienced people can often show you things you'd never see on your own, especially in a world of rapid technological change.

A strong circle is diverse in thought, united in values, and generous with encouragement. It doesn't echo everything you say; it challenges you to grow. Networking isn't just about making connections — it's about curating the ones that matter.

Practical Steps to Networking

Networking may sound lofty, but it's also practical. It's not about waiting for lightning to strike. It's about showing up with intention.

Start with clarity. What do you want? More clients? Personal growth? Mentorship? Your answer will shape your actions. Then, go where the people you want to meet actually are. That might be conferences, local meetups, community boards, or digital forums.

Don't rely only on digital connections. A "like" or comment on someone's post doesn't build a relationship. Show up in person when you can. Shake a hand, look someone in the eye, listen with focus.

After meeting someone, follow up. Send a note. Comment on something you discussed. Invite them to reconnect. Those small steps turn a handshake into a friendship.

Most importantly, contribute. Share opportunities, connect people to each other, offer your help. If you consistently add value, you'll always be remembered.

Networking Pitfalls to Avoid

Just as there are steps to do right, there are mistakes worth avoiding. Treating networking as a transaction — "What can I get from this person?" — kills trust instantly. People know when they're being used.

Another pitfall is inconsistency. If you only reach out when you need something, you haven't built a network; you've built a phonebook. Relationships require regular investment.

And finally, avoid the temptation to stay comfortable. It's easy to keep talking to the same people, in the same circles. But growth comes when you stretch into new spaces, new rooms, new conversations.

The Psychology of Connection

At the heart of networking is something deeply human: the desire to belong. Neuroscience tells us that connection activates the same reward centers in the brain as food or shelter. That's how important it is.

Networking isn't a business trick. It's human biology. We are wired to respond to generosity, to reciprocate kindness, to lean in when someone truly listens.

When you understand that, networking stops feeling like a chore. It starts feeling like what it really is: an opportunity to fulfill a basic human need — for you and for the person across from you.

The Future of Networking

As technology advances, networking is evolving. Social media, AI-driven platforms, and digital communities make it easier than ever to connect. But "easy" doesn't always mean "effective."

The future belongs to those who balance the digital with the personal. A message online may start a connection, but it's the phone call, the coffee, or the handshake that cements it. Authenticity will always outlast algorithms.

In the coming years, the best networkers will be those who harness technology to open doors but still walk through those doors in person.

A Philosophy to Live By

If I had to sum up everything I've learned about networking, it would be this: everyone you meet can teach you something.

That mindset changes everything. It makes every conversation an opportunity. It makes every stranger a potential ally. It makes every setback a chance to learn.

Networking isn't about deals or cards or handshakes. It's about curiosity, generosity, and authenticity. It's about building a circle of people who push you to grow while you do the same for them. It's about weaving a web of connections strong enough to catch you when you fall and launch you higher when you're ready to climb.

The beauty of networking is that it doesn't just change your business. It changes your life.

Conclusion

Networking is not a side activity. It's not a hobby. It's the multiplier that amplifies every other effort you make.

From coffee shop conversations to mastermind groups, from town council campaigns to national conferences, the principle is always the same: show up, give more than you take, and remember that every person you meet has something valuable to teach you.

So go out there. Start a conversation. Ask the question. Share the insight. Listen deeply.

And never forget:

"Your network is your net worth — not just in dollars, but in knowledge, in support, and in shared success."

Deepening the Practice of Networking

The longer I've been in business, the more I've realized that networking isn't something you "check off" a list. It's not like hitting the gym once and expecting to be in shape. It's a practice — ongoing, evolving, and strengthening with time.

Think about it this way: if you only reached out to your best friend once a year, how strong would that friendship be? Probably not very strong at all. Relationships require consistent care. It doesn't always have to be a big gesture — sometimes it's as simple as sending an encouraging text, sharing an article you know they'd like, or introducing them to someone in your circle. The small touchpoints, repeated over time, are what build unshakable trust.

One mistake I used to make was assuming networking only happened at "networking events." That couldn't be further from the truth. Networking happens every day, in the conversations you choose to start, the way you treat people in your community, the effort you put into staying in touch. If you start looking for opportunities to connect everywhere you go, you'll realize your network is much wider than you thought.

Networking Pitfalls, Revisited

Another pitfall I've seen over and over again is focusing too much on short-term gains. People walk into a room thinking, "Who here can buy from me?" instead of asking, "Who here can I learn from? Who here can I help?" That mindset shift makes all the difference.

I've also learned to beware of surface-level networking — the kind where you only know someone's title and company but nothing about who they are as a person. Those kinds of contacts rarely last. Instead, push yourself to go one step deeper. Ask about their story. What motivates them? What challenges are they facing? What do they do outside of work? Those are the conversations that lead to relationships.

Finally, don't underestimate the damage of neglect. If you build a relationship and then disappear until you need something, that's not networking — that's opportunism. True networking is about being present long before you ever ask for help.

The Future of Networking, Expanded

We're living in a time where networking is evolving faster than ever. Technology has made it possible to connect with thousands of people instantly, but the paradox is that people often feel more isolated and disconnected than before. That's why the future of networking won't just be about technology — it will be about how we use it with humanity.

Artificial intelligence may help us organize our contacts, remind us of birthdays, or even draft the first version of a follow-up email. These days, virtual reality even allows us to "attend" conferences with people across the globe without leaving our living rooms. These tools are exciting, but they can never replace the simple power of sitting across from someone, looking them in the eye, and listening.

The winners of the future will be those who embrace the tools but don't lose the touch. Those who combine digital reach with human warmth. Those who can send a quick DM but also pick up the phone, meet for coffee, or show up when it matters.

Final Reflection

If there's one truth I want to leave you with, it's this: networking is about people, not prospects. It's about connection, not collection. It's about building bridges, not burning them through business cards.

When you approach networking with that spirit — of generosity, curiosity, and persistence — you stop worrying about whether you're "doing it right." Because the truth is, the best networking doesn't feel like networking at all. It feels like friendship, like mentorship, like partnership. It feels like life, lived alongside others.

And in the end, that's what success is really about — not just what you achieve, but who you become and who you bring with you along the way.

Let's Network!

I'd love to connect with you and answer any questions you may have regarding this chapter.

You can follow me on Instagram @jamesbeaudoin6

Patricia Gagic is an internationally acclaimed contemporary artist, award-winning author, and successful entrepreneur from Canada. Her diverse career spans various fields, showcasing her multifaceted talents and dedication to both artistic expression and humanitarian causes. She is the world's leading wisdom-tradition-trained artist and meditation specialist, transforming high-achieving professionals to transmute karmic patterns, activate authentic core potential, and magnetize success through The Karmic Framework.

CHAPTER 5
Disrupting the Palette of Life by Noticing

by Patricia Karen Gagic
International Contemporary Artist, Founder
"Revived Expression Framework"

When you are born a soul with creativity as the elixir of life, you are handed one of the most challenging professions. It's like taking a walk into the *Dark Night of the Soul* without a compass, and finding the audience is paramount.

I am Patricia Gagic, and I have been internationally lauded as one of Canada's most exceptional communicators, an award-winning contemporary artist, author, percussionist, and entrepreneur. My journey spans from the corporate banking world to international art exhibitions, from Harvard Club speaking engagements to winning gold medals at the Carrousel du Louvre in Paris. But none of these achievements would have been possible without understanding one fundamental truth: networking is the empowerment that scales your exposure and gives voice to your creations.

This chapter explores how mindful networking—what I call "noticing"—can disrupt the ordinary palette of life and create extraordinary opportunities. Through my experiences transitioning from corporate executive to internationally recognized artist, I'll share how authentic connections, karmic awareness, and emotional intelligence can transform not just your career but your entire life trajectory.

The main insight I want to share is this: networking isn't about collecting business cards or making superficial connections. It's about showing up authentically, noticing opportunities with mindful awareness, and trusting that when you align your actions with your deepest purpose, the universe conspires to support your vision.

My networking journey began in earnest during a pivotal transition period in my life. After spending years in the corporate banking sector, where I had achieved my goal of becoming a bank manager before age twenty-five, my passion for photography and painting was taking over. This was the late 1990s, and I found myself at a crossroads many creative professionals face: how do you transition from a stable, well-defined career path to the uncertain, complex world of artistic expression?

The corporate world has taught me valuable lessons about systems, strategy, and the importance of community involvement. Many Fortune 500 companies mandate senior management to actively participate in local community organizations like United Way and Junior Achievement to establish a presence and goodwill. Since I was twelve years old, I had always been a volunteer with a sense of "service above self"—the Rotary motto that guided my actions. This made it effortless for me to jump in and get involved in various committee roles, including marketing, organizing golf tournaments, and supporting JA in Project Business.

My initial approach to networking in the art world was built on the foundation of genuine curiosity and service, which I had developed in my corporate career. I spent years volunteering for various organizations, which provided a Rolodex of contacts and, more importantly, taught me the value of giving before receiving.

The pivotal moment came when a friend reached out to suggest I connect with an artist in Toronto who was going to be exhibiting in Italy. This thoughtful gesture opened a door I hadn't even known existed. The concept of international exhibitions had been floating in my mind, but navigating the complexities of the art world seemed overwhelming. This single connection changed everything.

I learned early, the most powerful networking often comes through warm introductions from people who understand both your vision and the needs of others in their network. This wasn't about aggressive self-promotion; it was about allowing others to see value in facilitating meaningful connections.

Acting on that initial introduction, I made the decision to apply for the 2000 Biennale in Florence. I was accepted, and this became my first major international networking success. But the story that led to this moment reveals the mysterious nature of authentic networking.

The year before, in 1999, my husband had been consistently looking for a place in France to visit. Through another connection, I was introduced to a gallery in Toronto where I was invited to exhibit. While visiting the home of someone who would host us in France, I was invited to view their extensive art collection. Among all the breathtaking pieces, I was magically seduced by one painting named *Atila* by the artist Dragic.

When the owner mentioned that this artist lived about three hours from our destination in France, something profound stirred in me. Without overthinking, I asked if I could meet the artist. This single moment of courage, driven by genuine curiosity and artistic passion, would transform my entire career.

The Journey to Savoillan

The journey to meet Dragan Dragic in the summer of 1999 was itself a lesson in trusting the universe's timing. Savoillan is a small, isolated village lying at the foot of the north slope of Mont Ventoux, in the Sault area bordering both the Drome and the Alpes de Haute Provence. As our car wound through the increasingly remote countryside, I felt we were traveling not just geographically but spiritually into a realm where time moved differently.

Here you are in the land of lavender and spelt wheat. In July, when the lavender is in full bloom, the sight of the mauve fields speckled with golden wheat is magical. The landscape itself seemed to pulse with creative energy—endless rows of purple lavender stretching toward the imposing silhouette of Mont Ventoux, the ancient mountain that would become central to Dragic's artistic vision and, through him, to my own understanding of how place shapes artistic expression.

The village of Savoillan, with its population of fewer than 100 souls, felt like stepping into a medieval manuscript. Located in the Toulourenc valley, at the foot of the northern slope of the mythical Mont Ventoux, Savoillan is a small, isolated village between the mountains and the meadows, in absolute calm. Stone houses clustered around narrow streets, their weathered walls telling stories of centuries past. The sound of the Toulourenc River provided a constant, gentle soundtrack to our approach.

What I didn't know then was that the contemporary painter Dragan Dragic had lived in Savoillan for almost 40 years. The landscapes of the Ventoux have always been a great source of inspiration for him. For nearly four decades, this Serbian-born master had chosen this remote corner of Provence as his sanctuary, allowing the stark beauty of Mont Ventoux and the intimate scale of village life to infuse his work with a unique blend of grandeur and intimacy.

The Master's Sanctuary

Finding Dragic's atelier required asking directions from villagers who spoke of him with a mixture of pride and reverence. His studio wasn't hidden in a village of 90 inhabitants, nothing truly could be—but it felt protected by the landscape itself, nestled against the hillside as if it had grown from the earth.

When I first crossed the threshold of his workspace, I was struck by the contradiction between the rustic simplicity of the village and the sophistication of what lay before me. Dragan Dragic had an artistic career marked by high standards. He studied art in his native Serbia before coming to France in 1971. He then worked with great artists such as Bernard Buffet, Marc Chagall, and Victor Vasarely. The posters on his walls weren't boastful displays but quiet testimonies to a life dedicated to artistic excellence.

The studio itself was a temple to the creative process. Canvases in various stages of completion lined the walls, each one revealing his evolution toward his abstract and lyrical style that characterizes him today. Natural light poured through north-facing windows, illuminating palettes heavy with pigments that seemed to capture the very essence of the Provençal landscape outside.

But it was Dragic himself who commanded the space. Born in Serbia in 1944, he carried himself with the quiet authority of someone who had spent decades in pursuit of artistic truth. His English was non-existent—his French was careful but warm— and I sensed immediately that this was a man who understood the difference between technique and artistry, between making pictures and creating vision.

The Master's Teaching

What followed were not traditional art lessons but immersions in a philosophy of seeing. It was in the 1980s that he developed his abstract and lyrical style, and he was generous in sharing not just techniques but the intellectual and spiritual journey that had led him to this distinctive voice.

"Look," he would say, gesturing toward Mont Ventoux visible through his studio windows. Dragan Dragic had a fascination for Mont Ventoux, this emblematic mountain of the Vaucluse region. He dedicated many works to it, where he sought to represent the purity and strength of this majestic nature. For him, the mountain wasn't merely a subject but a meditation on permanence and change, on the relationship between the eternal and the momentary.

He taught me to see color not as decoration but as emotion made visible. His palette knife moved across the canvas with the precision of a surgeon and the passion of a poet. Watching him work, I began to understand that technique without soul produces mere illustration, while soul without technique produces only frustration.

The weeks I spent traveling back and forth between Canada and Savoillan became a pilgrimage of sorts. Each journey deepened my understanding not just of painting but of what it means to live as an artist. Dragic showed me how to prepare canvases with the reverence of a monk illuminating manuscripts, how to mix colors until they sang with life, how to know when a painting was finished—not when it looked right, but when it felt complete.

The Village as Classroom

Savoillan is right off the beaten track, in complete stillness, away from the major roads. This isolation, which might have felt limiting to some, created the perfect environment for deep learning. Without the distractions of urban life, every moment became an opportunity to observe, to absorb, to understand.

The rhythm of village life became part of my artistic education. Morning light on ancient stone walls taught me about the subtlety of shadows. The way lavender fields shifted color throughout the day showed me how light could transform the same landscape into infinite variations. Even simple conversations with villagers—the baker, the postmistress, the elderly men who gathered in the café—taught me about the kind of authentic human connection that great art seeks to capture.

Dragic often spoke about his constant search for purity and simplicity in his works. Living temporarily in Savoillan, I began to understand what he meant. In a place where life was stripped down to essentials—good food, meaningful work, genuine community—art, too, could achieve a kind of clarity impossible in more complex environments.

The Transformation

Those weeks in Savoillan transformed not just my artistic technique but my understanding of what networking truly means. Here was a master artist, internationally recognized, who had chosen to make his life in one of the most remote villages in France. Yet his influence radiated outward through the work of students like me, through exhibitions in galleries, through the simple fact of living his art with complete integrity.

Dragic taught me that authentic networking isn't about expanding your circle—it's about deepening your center. When you become genuinely excellent at what you do, when you live your values with consistency, when you approach your work with both humility and confidence, the right connections find you. He never actively promoted himself, yet collectors, curators, and fellow artists sought him out in his mountain village.

This became one of the most profound networking relationships of my life. For twenty-five years now, this extraordinary gentleman has graced me with his genius, knowledge, friendship, skills, and connections. But more than that, he showed me how to be the kind of artist—and person—that others want to learn from and work with.

The generosity of spirit in mentorship spilled into my existence, and I rose to shield the integrity of mastery. In Savoillan, surrounded by lavender fields and ancient stones, under the watchful presence of Mont Ventoux, I learned that the highest form of networking is teaching others to surpass you.

The prophetic timing continued to unfold. Armed with new confidence and a Matisse-adjusted palette, I was prepared for two major events. The exhibition in Italy opened channels for networks of connections that would never have occurred if I hadn't been prepared, harnessed the opportunity, and maintained the most congruent attitude imaginable.

While in Florence, the connection with the Toronto artist led to another pivotal moment. She had been invited to meet with organizers of an art fair in Switzerland and asked if I would like to take the train from Florence to Milan and then to Caslano, Switzerland—all in one day. Without hesitation, I said yes.

This meeting proved fortuitous as the organizers loved my work and invited me to participate in several future events in Berlin, Geneva, and Zurich. One day of courageous networking led to years of international opportunities.

Lessons Learned

Authentic Curiosity Over Agenda: The most effective networking strategy I discovered was approaching connections with genuine curiosity rather than a predetermined agenda. When I saw Dragic's painting, I wasn't thinking about career advancement; I was genuinely moved by the art and wanted to meet the creator. This authentic interest created a foundation for a relationship that has lasted decades.

Service-First Mindset: My years of volunteer work have taught me that the most sustainable networking comes from a service-first mindset. Whether working on United Way campaigns or community art projects, I focused on contributing value before seeking benefit. This approach built trust and genuine relationships that naturally led to opportunities.

Mindful Observation and "Noticing": I developed what I call the art of "noticing"—mindful observation without judgment. This involves stepping away from your own thoughts and simply evaluating situations and people without immediate definition or categorization. This skill allows me to recognize opportunities and connections others might miss.

Emotional Intelligence and Self-Awareness: Several years ago, I made one of the smartest decisions of my life by enrolling in the Transformative Mindfulness and Applied Mindfulness programs at the University of Toronto. These three-year programs catalyzed my self-awareness and deepened my understanding of meditation, clarity, and purification, which support emotional capacity.

When we recognize the patterns of our emotions, we can transform how we approach decision-making, relationships, and leadership capacity. Developing good networking skills requires this same level of emotional intelligence. It's not enough to show up and meet people. If we lack confidence in ourselves and our offerings, we won't be noticed.

Adaptation and Learning: I learned to adapt my networking style based on opportunities, feedback, and desired results. The corporate networking I had mastered was different from the artistic community networking I needed to develop. Being willing to learn and adjust my approach while maintaining my authentic core was crucial.

The networking journey, which began with a simple introduction to a Toronto artist, led to extraordinary business outcomes that transformed my entire career trajectory. The international connections I made through authentic relationship-building resulted in:

Global Exhibition Opportunities: My work has been exhibited in Florence, Berlin, Geneva, Zurich, and Paris, with my networking relationships directly facilitating each opportunity. The Swiss organizers I met through the Toronto artist connection became long-term partners who opened doors across Europe.

Prestigious Recognition: I won the Salon National des Beaux-Arts Gold Medal at the Carrousel du Louvre in Paris and received the Silver, Pewter, and Vermeil Medal from the Academique Societe Arts Sciences Lettres of France. These achievements came from networks within networks—relationships that led to introductions that led to opportunities.

Speaking Engagements: My networking led to invitations to speak at prestigious venues, including the Harvard Club of Boston, Carnegie Hall, and NASDAQ. Each speaking opportunity came through personal connections who believed in my message and wanted to share it with their networks.

Media and Documentation: A documentary on my art career was released by Vividarts Network (vividarts.tv) in 2024, and ATIM Art Tour International named me Artist of the Year in both 2020 and 2023. These opportunities emerged from relationships built over years of authentic networking.

Business Partnerships: The connections I made led to co-founding the Reflections Initiative, supporting children in Cambodia and Nicaragua. This meaningful work emerged from relationships with people who shared my values and wanted to create a positive impact together.

Personal Growth: The networking journey fundamentally changed who I am as a person, developing skills and perspectives that extend far beyond professional success.

Personal Development

Confidence and Authentic Self-Expression: Initially, I struggled with the question, "Am I good enough?" Through networking experiences that consistently validated my authentic self-expression, I developed unshakeable confidence in my artistic vision and my ability to communicate it effectively.

Emotional Intelligence and Mindfulness: The networking challenges I faced drove me to develop deeper emotional intelligence through formal mindfulness training. I learned to regulate my emotional responses, create healthy boundaries, and make decisions from a place of clarity rather than fear or urgency.

Cultural Competence and Global Perspective: Networking across international boundaries exposed me to different cultural approaches to business, art, and relationship-building. This expanded my worldview and made me more effective at connecting with people from diverse backgrounds.

Leadership and Mentorship: As my network grew, I naturally evolved into a mentor and leader for other artists. The generosity of spirit that Dragic showed me became a model for how I now support emerging creatives in their networking journeys.

Karmic Awareness: Perhaps most significantly, I developed what I call "karmic awareness"—the understanding that authentic networking is about showing up to what you consciously believe, creating a beacon of confidence that attracts the right opportunities without being in active pursuit.

Challenges

Overcoming Introversion and Social Anxiety: I was once called a "converted introvert," though I sense I'm simply a complicated extrovert with comfortable passivity. Not all of us are naturally comfortable in networking zones, and I had to develop strategies for managing social anxiety while maintaining authenticity.

The emotional intelligence work I did through the University of Toronto programs was crucial here. When we are in urgent or forced situations, we have little time to honor our feelings or process our emotions, leading to rushed decisions. Learning to check in with myself regularly allowed me to rebalance and make better networking decisions.

Managing Judgment and Public Visibility: When you are seen in public, there is an automatic sense of being judged, which can feel uncomfortable, especially when you value others' opinions. Most of my networking challenges stemmed from my own insecurities rather than external obstacles.

I had to learn that networking is a skill that improves with practice. As I became more confident, the flow became more authentic and engaging. Trust built naturally, and relationships began to thrive.

Financial and Logistical Challenges: The art world presents unique networking challenges involving money and logistics. Traveling, shipping costs, marketing, and fees all become part of the decision-making process for each networking opportunity. Unlike corporate networking, where companies often cover expenses, artists must invest their own resources in building relationships.

I learned to reach out to friends and family who lived abroad, creating a cushion of support. Their commitment inspired my confidence that this was indeed my job, and the investment was worthwhile.

Navigating Different Cultural Contexts: International networking requires learning to adapt to different cultural approaches to relationship-building. What worked in Canadian corporate culture didn't necessarily translate to European art communities or international business settings.

Developing Emotional Boundaries: Through my mindfulness training, I learned to create emotional boundaries, which are especially important since my undefined Solar Plexus makes me prone to absorbing others' emotions. I developed practices for:

- Regular emotional check-ins to maintain balance
- Embracing the full spectrum of emotions without judgment
- Avoiding major decisions during emotional extremes
- Seeking clarity and calm before making important networking choices

Building Authentic Confidence: Rather than trying to project false confidence, I learned to build authentic confidence through preparation and genuine expertise. The weeks I spent with Dragic, paying attention to every detail of technique and artistry, gave me legitimate confidence in my abilities.

Strategic Investment in Relationships: I learned to view networking investments strategically, understanding that some relationships require significant time and financial investment before bearing fruit. The key was choosing investments aligned with my authentic vision rather than chasing every opportunity.

Do's and Don'ts for Effective Networking

Do:

- Approach networking with authentic curiosity rather than predetermined agendas
- Invest time in developing emotional intelligence and self-awareness
- Practice mindful observation—"noticing"—without immediate judgment
- Give value before seeking benefit through service-oriented activities
- Prepare thoroughly so you can show up with genuine confidence
- Follow up consistently and maintain long-term relationship perspectives
- Trust karmic timing while taking appropriate action

Don't:

- Network only when you need something—build relationships consistently
- Ignore your emotional state when making networking decisions

- Try to be someone you're not to impress others
- Expect immediate returns on relationship investments
- Neglect the importance of deep, meaningful connections for superficial quantity
- Let fear of judgment prevent you from authentic self-expression
- Underestimate the power of seemingly small connections

The Power of Karmic Networking

My deepest learning is about what I call "karmic networking"—the understanding that when you show up authentically to what you consciously believe, you create a beacon that attracts the right opportunities and people. This isn't passive waiting; it's active alignment with your deepest purpose, combined with openness to unexpected pathways.

Reflecting on Impact

Networking has transformed my life in ways I could never have imagined when I made that first inquiry about meeting Dragic. What began as curiosity about a painting on someone's wall led to a 25-year mentorship, international recognition, and a completely transformed career. More importantly, it led to deep personal growth, meaningful relationships, and the ability to create positive impact through various initiatives.

The ripple effects continue to expand. Each authentic connection I made led to others, creating a web of relationships that supports not just my artistic career, but my growth as a human being. The emotional intelligence I developed through networking challenges made me a better leader, mentor, and community member.

As I look forward, my approach to networking continues to evolve. I'm increasingly focused on mentorship and supporting other artists in their networking journeys, sharing the generous spirit that Dragic showed me. The networks I've built over decades are now platforms for creating positive change and supporting emerging talent.

I'm also exploring how digital technologies can enhance authentic networking without replacing the deep, personal connections that have been so transformative in my journey. The principles remain the same—authenticity, service, mindful awareness—but the tools and platforms continue to expand.

If you're reading this and are feeling overwhelmed by the prospect of networking, especially if you're transitioning careers or pursuing creative work, I want you to know that networking isn't about becoming someone you're not. It's about becoming more authentically who you are and trusting that the right people will be drawn to your authenticity.

Start where you are, with genuine curiosity about others and a willingness to serve. Practice the art of "noticing"—mindful observation without judgment. Invest in your emotional intelligence and self-awareness. Most importantly, trust that when you align your networking efforts with your deepest purpose and values, extraordinary opportunities will emerge.

The network effect isn't just about professional success—it's about creating a life of meaning, connection, and positive impact. Every conversation is an opportunity to practice authenticity, every connection a chance to serve others, every relationship a pathway to mutual growth and transformation.

Your authentic voice matters. The world needs what you have to offer. Trust the process, show up fully, and allow networking to become not just a professional tool, but a pathway to a life of deeper purpose and connection.

Remember: you are exactly where you have chosen to be, and you have the gift of time to accelerate your vision. The universe is waiting for you to show up.

Jacob Godar is an expert at growing profi table lawn care and landscaping companies and helping others scale their service businesses to seven fi gures.

Business Coach
GROW Comm Host
GROW by Design podcast
CEO, Scooter's Lawn Care, Inc.

Connect with me at:
https://www.jacobgodar.com/

CHAPTER 6

Staying Uncomfortable: The Relentless Advantage of Growth Through Networking

I'm Jacob Godar, a father, husband, and the founder of a lawn and landscape company that has grown from homemade door hangers to a successful multi-state operation. Looking back, I always knew I wanted to do something big—and I still believe I will do something big.

But haven't you already?

Sure, I have accomplished some impressive things in my life so far, but there is still so much more I can do. That mindset is what keeps me striving for the next level in business—and what fuels my excitement every single day. Each day is another opportunity to see what I can accomplish and what new value I can bring to the world. Who can I meet, and how can we collaborate?

Funny enough, I am writing this chapter because of the very lesson this book talks about. The person who invited me to contribute here is someone I met at a conference seven years ago. That is the beauty of networking. It is a long-term investment and not always an immediate return—a powerful tool that will continue to give back, often when we least expect it.

SECTION 1: The Ceiling We All Hit

In 2017, I hit a ceiling. The lawn care and landscaping company I had built from the ground up in central Illinois was stable. I relocated my family to southwest Florida and opened a second location there, but it was operating out of our home. I felt stuck. I was struggling with a scarcity mindset: fear around money, fear around growth. I needed a mindset shift. Books, Audible, YouTube, and online forums were not enough anymore. I needed real people in my corner.

I realize we all hit ceilings. It might not be money for you. It could be fear of failure or judgment. If you do not find a way around it, that wall will wear you down. First comes burnout. Then comes quitting on your dream. That is why it is so important to me to share this: I have been where you are—or where you soon could find yourself. You will encounter roadblocks, walls, ceilings— whatever you want to call them—in any endeavor you pursue. My goal is to give you tools to break through them, time and time again.

Takeaway: Every level of growth has a ceiling—but these ceilings are meant to be shattered, not lived under.

SECTION 2: Scarcity, Fear, and the Stories We Inherit

Before I started my company, people told me, "It used to be easier to get a business up and running." I believed it—not because I had proof, but because I truly did not know any better. Would it even be worth it to try? When you do not know what is possible, it is easy to inherit doubt. People will tell you things from their own limited point of view, from behind their own walls of fear. My advice? Only listen to the people who are exactly where you want to be. Do not listen to those too scared to try. Those people can misguide you, even if their intentions are pure.

Each time you listen to the wrong person, a seed of doubt is planted in your mind. Small at first, but these seeds can grow into very real limitations. These seeds planted scarcity in my own life: fear of losing my business before it had a chance to thrive; fear of failing as a husband, father, and leader. My fears were not just stalling my business growth—they were hurting the people I loved. It was time to take action.

I started my mission to rewrite my self-limiting stories in 2018 at Tony Robbins' *Unleash the Power Within* event. This event transformed my mindset and shifted the trajectory of my personal and professional growth. It was intense, and the lessons I learned there made it clear: this will be a lifelong effort to rewrite the stories that no longer serve me, over and over again.

Takeaway: If the story you are living is no longer serving you, rewrite it—starting with who you listen to.

SECTION 3: The First Fire Walk

Unleash the Power Within changed my life. If you ever have the opportunity to go to this event, do it. It lasted 12–14 hours a day. At around 2:30 a.m. on the first night, I walked across burning coals with 10,000 other people. It was symbolic, intense, and completely unforgettable. I met phenomenal people, and I was excited to start nurturing connections. Most importantly, this event achieved exactly what I needed at the time: I was starting to break down my own walls and rewrite the stories that were keeping me stuck and afraid to move forward.

Interestingly, this was not my first time walking on fire. Years earlier, before I ever started my own business, my mentor and then-boss sent me to Discover Leadership, a personal development event. It was jarring right out of the gate. It challenged my thinking, broke me down, and built me back up.

They told us to yell at the top of our lungs. It forced us out of our comfort zones. And yes, you guessed it—the final rite of passage at this event was a fire walk. Discover Leadership planted a seed: discomfort is a doorway. I have been walking eagerly through these doors ever since.

People tell me I look calm under pressure, that I do not appear stressed when making important business decisions. The truth? I am terrified. I have found that is the secret to business—and all of life. Courage and fear can co-exist, but they cannot exist 50/50. They must exist 51/49. Be afraid, but be brave enough to do it anyway. Maybe that is all that separates me from those that cautioned against risk and warned me that "it used to be easier" to be a business owner. People seek comfort, but success is uncomfortable. Growth hurts.

Takeaway: Courage isn't the absence of fear. It's doing the thing anyway—especially when the coals are hot.

SECTION 4: When the Room Changes You

At the end of *Unleash the Power Within*, the Tony Robbins event team was pitching tickets to the next event: *Business Mastery*. Where the first event helped me break down stories of self-doubt, this event would take my business to the next level—guaranteed. The big pitch? If you do not get a million dollars' worth of value on the first day, you can walk out and get a 100% refund. Sounds like a dream for a struggling business owner, right? Wrong. A single ticket cost $10,000.

I remember this moment like it was yesterday. I stepped outside to call my wife. With two babies in her arms and no hesitation, she said, "Get back in there before you run out of time."

Did I lose you? You are probably thinking, "It must be nice to say your business was 'stuck,' but you were still able to afford a

$10,000 ticket." I couldn't. I charged it to a nearly maxed-out line of credit. I was terrified. That's the point.

Business Mastery changed my life as a business owner, which in turn—and without a doubt—accelerated my business growth. This event showed me that none of this is about the event.

It put me in the room with the people I was aching to meet. I met people who were exactly where I wanted to be. I met people who were on the same journey there. Every conversation I had was important. I was either absorbing knowledge from someone way smarter than me or empathizing with someone in the same trenches. For me, this event was about networking and the connections I could make with people like me, just a few steps further ahead. It was about the power an event has to bring together a group of people.

As an ambitious entrepreneur, it can be hard to build a network like this. It can rarely be found in our families or lifelong friends; they serve a different, equally important purpose in our lives. Even if you live in a big city, it can be difficult to build this type of network. Events are packed with people who all want the exact same thing: massive growth in their personal, professional, and financial lives. These people are excited about it, on fire with ideas, and willing to talk for hours. Some of the best times are the post-event dinners and drinks, brainstorming limitless possibilities for each of you.

This is where conferences can make a massive impact in building your network. Tony Robbins' events specifically force attendees to get to know each other, so you can't escape the networking part.

I was terrified to spend $10,000 that I did not have. But with my wife's support and my commitment to rewriting my own stories of scarcity, I attended an event that showed me that you cannot put a price tag on the right network. I directly attribute this event to the successful move to my company's first commercial location. This move did not make sense on paper. The rent was $3,700 per month with a three-year commitment. It was out of my budget. How could I make this happen? But I decided to rewrite my story at this moment and take the risk. This expansion pushed our company to one million dollars in annual revenue.

As my network was expanding, I was starting to gain perspective. My big, scary risk was just another Tuesday afternoon for someone else. When you meet someone who is spending one million dollars per month on Facebook ads, you ask yourself: Why am I so afraid of things that seem so small in comparison? I used these moments as a motivator to push myself further, and now my company is thriving at over five million dollars in annual sales.

Takeaway: Growth accelerates when you put yourself in rooms where it is normal to think big.

SECTION 5: Belief by Association

Until this point, I had spent years growing a business, but I had never done it before. I had no proof that I could do this. I was simply asking my family and friends to believe in me. As you probably know, it felt like it could crash and burn at any time. Part of me felt like some of them were waiting to watch me fail.

So when I started building relationships with people I met at events, I was astounded at the immediate belief each of them had in me. I had not pitched or proven myself to them. And still, there were perfect strangers: offering moral support because they had been exactly where I was at the time, or because they were there at that moment, too. I found an instant community— and even investors.

At one event several years ago, I was sharing my struggles with a new acquaintance. I told him that our southwest Florida location was still new and burning cash fast. We had $150,000 on our line of credit and a $115,000 credit card bill due. I was scared. I felt like I was making all the wrong decisions—and at this point, it was more than just my own family's livelihood on the line. Florida was growing, but our Illinois location was shut down for the winter, so no money was coming in there. After explaining all of this, I said, "I have money in the market that would at least clear my line of credit and most of the credit card, if it really came down to it." He looked me square in the eye and said, "It sounds like you're barely taking any risk at all." That one little comment reframed the entire situation in my mind. He was right. It wasn't really that bad, and there was a way out. Shortly after, he came to me and said, "When you're ready to push harder, I'll invest." Even though we never struck a deal, this interaction set me on fire and helped rebuild my confidence.

I have had these kinds of experiences over and over at events—always getting little nuggets that helped me grow, always building that next right connection that picked me back up, helped me go further—and usually even faster. Proximity has power, so make sure you are around the right people. Jim Rohn was right: you will end up the average of the five people you spend the most time with.

Takeaway: Surround yourself with people who believe in your potential more than you believe in your past.

SECTION 6: Go Alone to Grow

If you want to make the greatest impact, go alone to your next event. Show up in a place where you know absolutely no one, and start meeting people. So often I see people show up with a friend and then use that friend as a life raft. You both, maybe even unintentionally, create an echo chamber and hear less new voices and opinions. Ultimately, the new voices are the gold—and exactly what you should be listening for at each event. Every time I have invited a team member to an event, I have received less in an effort to make them feel more comfortable and at ease.

If you must go to an event with someone you know (even your significant other), it is very important for each of you to set a clear intention. What do you want to get from this event? What is the one takeaway you each so desperately need right now to expand? Remember that you are not just going to hang out together, especially if that means skipping the networking after-parties. You are going to this event in order to expand your thinking and build connections. Go your separate ways. Spend time with new people. Have new conversations with people who see things differently. When you take this advice, you are sure to find the gold at any event.

Takeaway: Going alone might feel uncomfortable—but comfort zones don't build connection or confidence.

SECTION 7: The One Idea Rule

You are always one person and one idea away from changing your entire life. Life is all about timing. Think about all of those moments in your life where if you showed up just one moment later, everything would be different. That is what each networking event should be treated like—a "blink and you'll miss it" opportunity. Swing at every conversation, every connection, because you might miss—but you will never hit if you don't start swinging.

Sure, you will face obstacles. It is not always easy to walk into a room, especially by yourself. You can be afraid to start conversations (remember, you only have to be 51% brave). Even though you know that business owners love helping other business owners, it can still be uncomfortable to strike up a conversation with a stranger. What if that business owner looks like they are more successful than you? It may feel downright impossible to approach them. Then you have ultimately lost out on an opportunity—and what if that person could have changed your entire life?

Another major takeaway is something we all struggle with as excited entrepreneurs: listen to hear, not just to respond. Be interesting, but be even more interested. Be interested in everyone you meet—who they are, what they do, and where they're going. Learn to enjoy others' excitement as well. It will make your relationships even deeper and help you better understand the people around you.

Takeaway: You are always one conversation, one person, or one idea away from changing everything.

Final Thoughts: Keep Walking through the Fire

Each time I leave an event, I feel like a super-charged battery. I buzz for weeks. I become reinvigorated to show up for my family, grow my business, and generate even more opportunity for my team. I leave with deeper relationships and new contacts to nurture. I fill a notebook with notes, but my main takeaway from every event is always the same. I will continue to pay thousands of dollars to leave each event with this exact same takeaway.

My Takeaway: I am going to be the best father and husband. I will be the best provider, leader of the family, and rock in their corner. I will be the best person I can be for the people who matter most to me.

Have you ever heard from your loved ones that your business drains you? That they can see how difficult it is for you? Of course, we as business owners are used to living with the weight of owning a business through all of its glorious ups and downs— but when our loved ones can see the toll it takes, it should be a wake-up call. It usually isn't. So when I come back from an event feeling electrified and motivated, the feeling is contagious throughout my home. I appreciate my family even more, and they give that energy right back to me. Maybe it is different for each person, but for me it is simple: a reminder of how grateful I am that they trust me to be their provider.

What is the point of this life anyway, except to be there for others? This thinking can transcend into our home, friendships, and business. All of my relationships—all of these beautiful networks I have built through the years—have shown a mirror on who I want to be. I do not want to build this life and then never have a moment to enjoy it—or have anyone to enjoy it with.

As I write this, I have already booked my next Tony Robbins event. I am still learning. Still networking, still walking through the fire. My hope is that reading this inspires you to keep walking through fires every day, to keep doing the big, scary things that make you feel uncomfortable.

Moving forward in my life, I am excited to keep leveraging the tools that events can provide. We get this one at-bat in life, and we get the opportunity to make the best of it. Do not get complacent though; at new levels, there are new devils. Your business will get bigger, and you will have growing pains. Your life will get bigger, and you may grow away from people. But if you are on this path, you can align with others that are on the same road—either next to you or further ahead. Networking can become your lifeline—your people and your tribe, the chosen family you have built to confide in when nowhere else seems safe. This life is filled with suffering, and that is an important and beautiful part of it—but the right people can make it easier to suffer well.

CYNTHIA MANION is an author, model, actress and bodybuilder who is passionate about helping women over 60 reinvent themselves in order to achieve more joyful (and healthier) lives.

A former swimsuit model (**Oscar de la Renta**) who was named "Mrs. New York America" in 1993, Cynthia loves helping women feel powerful and she believes in the connection between working out (weight-lifting, yoga) and leading a happy life.

Cynthia is the author of two books: The Amazon Best-Seller, *Savannah Seas: Maiden Voyage (The Savannah Valley Series)* and *Black Pearl: A Love Letter to the Ocean*, both of which feature female characters who are strong and focused on living their best life. She is also the host of the weekly podcast, "The Cynthia Manion Show."

CHAPTER 7
From Runway Model to Business Leader

Ever since I was a young girl, frequently moving all over the world as my United States Air Force Lieutenant Colonel father was transferred to assignments, I've been learning the art of building genuine connections. At that age, being 'The New Girl', I HAD to figure out how to make friends and exist. I didn't know then that's what we call 'networking' in the business world. From Europe to East Africa to the Seychelles Islands to the U.S.A., each new place taught me how to quickly establish authentic relationships in any environment.

Little did I know then that these early "people skills" would become the foundation of my business success, leading to multimillion-dollar deals with companies like Harley Davidson and transforming me from a model fitting clothes and walking the runway for Oscar de la Renta into a national sales manager building lasting business relationships.

But here's the thing - networking isn't about the deals. It's about the people. In my journey from fashion model to business leader, I've discovered that the most powerful business relationships aren't built in boardrooms - they're built on genuine human connections that transform vendors into trusted partners, and clients into lifelong friends. Let me share with you the three most important lessons I've learned about creating these lasting business relationships through authentic networking. Without giving away any spoilers, here's a hint: It's NOT about tactics, gimmicks, or processes. Processes are taught in business - yes, they are important. But that's just "sheet music" for effective networking. You're about to learn three crucial insights for playing 'music' like a world-class musician. Ready?

Lesson Number 1: The Client Always Comes First - Always

The most important thing about networking - and I mean this with every fiber of my being - is to keep the client in mind. Not your commission. Not your quota. Not your ego. The client.

I believe that I've succeeded because I only cared about the client, their needs, and what served them. I have never done anything that wasn't in their best interest - for them or my company. One, it helped me sleep at night. Two, in the long run, it gave me more clients and more business.

That mindset means being strong internally. How do you leap over the trap of pushing a sale when your rent or mortgage is due? I've struggled through that, too. It meant sticking to my values, to who I really am, then doing what I knew was right.

That started with moving to New York City with only $450.00, a very used car, and a mattress strapped to my roof, which put me in exactly that situation. After renting an apartment for $400.00, I needed to find a job fast. So, I focused on doing the work and following the process for finding work. As a professional model, that meant literally visiting every modeling agency in New York, starting with "A" in an industry business directory. I wore out my high heels, but landed a job when I got midway through "I" on the list, after two and a half weeks. Was that networking? Not exactly. It was sticking to my goals and values. Staying focused. Trying times like that build the habits and the belief that carries you through those tempting moments when bills - and other pressures - could push you to do the easy but wrong thing.

Let me share another story that perfectly illustrates this principle. One of my best clients - they became number one, actually - went through three different decision-makers during our business relationship. Now, most vendors would panic at that kind of turnover. Instead, because of the groundwork I created in the beginning, by focusing entirely on their needs, each new decision-maker simply accepted that I was "the girl." Why? Because I had become part of their family.

I don't mean that figuratively. I was invited to their Thanksgivings, their Bar Mitzvahs, Bat Mitzvahs, birthdays, weddings, and their building openings - often as the only vendor present. It's freaking amazing! But it happened because I never went in desperate for a sale. Instead, I went in as a consultant, trying to understand what was truly needed, or if they even needed my services at all. Sometimes it wasn't a fit at that time.

Take my experience with an organization that works with disabled individuals. When they faced significant operational challenges, I didn't see dollar signs - I saw people who needed help. I practically lived there, visiting almost daily to figure out exactly what they needed. When my own company initially said "no" to their requirements, I pushed back hard. "This is what they need," I insisted. "I've got to figure it out."

That resulted in thinking so far out of the box I was in a different room! We didn't offer some of the services the organization needed, so I bundled in outsourced IT components they needed. We got the business but gave up some short-term profit. However, the long business relationship that resulted gave us far more profit than an "average" account. Was it more work for me? Absolutely. But it was what the client needed, and that's what mattered.

Lesson Number 2: Treat Everyone Like They're the CEO

Here's something that might surprise you - some of my most valuable business relationships weren't with decision-makers. They were with receptionists, maintenance staff, and the people most often ignored. Why? Because in my experience, when you treat everyone the same, whether they're CEO or janitor, magical things happen!

Of course, I know who the decision maker is - the CEO, the president - often getting their blessings first, and who will sign the contract and checks. Then I research everything I can on the people. While that helps with building a relationship, especially where we have common interests, it's not enough. Decision makers are surrounded by people who will enthusiastically support doing business with you, OR just as loudly undermine your opportunities … .a chorus of "no". They can't say yes, but they can certainly veto your deal or muddy it up.

At the client just described above, I didn't just know the CEO, IT director, and primary decision-makers. I knew everyone. When I walked in, people would light up with "Hi Cynthia!" There was one gentleman there - he had an incredible memory for dates - who would tell me everything that happened on my birthday every single time he saw me. Some people might have rushed past him to get to "more important" meetings. I would stand there and listen to him for twenty minutes, appreciating his unique gift and learning from his knowledge.

Let me tell you a story about why this matters. I had a major delivery of a few dozen copiers - that's what I was selling at the time - in a new building, on the top floor, in a construction zone. Everything was lined up perfectly except for one small detail - we needed after-hours elevator access. Now, if I had been one of those vendors who only spoke to the C-suite, we would have been dead in the water. But I had built a relationship with the janitor. Somebody, that's too often invisible to the "suits," yet no less a professional in his domain. I simply "saw" him, took time to learn his name, and then talked with him whenever we crossed paths. Well, because of that, he unlocked those elevators for me after hours, and we got everything done. My client was beyond happy!

Sometimes I had potential clients that other salespeople didn't want. Taking care of customers that people considered lowly - that's how others might see it. But here's the truth: there are no unimportant people. Everyone matters, and when you genuinely believe that and act on it, your network becomes unbreakable.

And here's a bonus secret. It's fun! You would not believe how satisfying it is to bring in a sale from one of those new clients.

Lesson Number 3: Go Above and Beyond - But Keep It Real

The third lesson I've learned is about exceeding expectations while staying authentic. This isn't about grand gestures for show - it's about genuine commitment to excellence and service.

Let me give you an example. When implementing a new system for a client, I didn't just deliver the technical solution. I organized a comprehensive rollout that included providing lunch for 500 people - on my own dime, over a few thousand dollars. I had balloons, welcome signs, and my entire staff stationed at copiers for two days, working in shifts to ensure everyone got proper training.

Why? Well, have you ever experienced a software upgrade or bought a new gadget that seemed so simple to use during the sales presentation, BUT got extremely frustrated when you attempted to use it? Imagine having a trainer from the selling company in your office, guiding you on how to use it, then answering all the questions you have once you start using it - for no extra charge. How do you feel about that vendor?

But there's still more to the story! I organized the training sessions by department so people could ask questions comfortably and focus on the features most relevant to their work. Was all this necessary? Strictly speaking, no. But it ensured the implementation's success and showed everyone they mattered. Meanwhile, they have gone through three CEOs and two IT regimes, yet they are still a client, and they still invite me to their Gala every year!

Here's another story that illustrates this principle. I was at MAGIC (a fashion tradeshow) in LA as a new Harley-Davidson representative - yes, the motorcycle company. They have an incredible clothing merchandising operation. I had lined up potential client appointments for the entire convention. When one of my clients showed up, instead of focusing on sales tactics, I spent time genuinely connecting with him about his family and motorcycle interests. We barely discussed business at all. The result? He wrote me an order for a million dollars and walked away like it was nothing.

My people couldn't believe it. They had their jaws on the ground. I didn't even look at the order - I just helped him get what he wanted, and I didn't even know what quantities he was putting down. When everyone was whooping and hollering, I wanted to say, "Act like we've been here before. You guys are embarrassing me." It revealed they didn't really believe we could get an order that big. But I did. So did our new client.

Do you truly believe that about your company? About yourself?

Here's a bonus lesson: Networking is an "inside job." It will reveal to you and your prospects what your really deeply held beliefs are. If that reveals you don't really like people or don't believe in what you are doing...well, start there and fix that before applying the three lessons we've been discussing here.

The Results of Real Relationships

This approach to networking - focusing on genuine relationships, treating everyone with respect, and going above and beyond while staying authentic - has led to remarkable business success. But more importantly, it's created lasting relationships that continue long after business engagements end.

Client contacts tend to take jobs elsewhere. Guess who the preferred vendor is at that new company? That's right, I am, because of the deep relationship I've built with that person. Does that happen every time? Of course not. It has contributed to my being the "Salesperson of the Month" most months.

Many of my clients have become true friends over the years. I still receive invitations to galas and events from organizations I worked with years ago. Former clients send me Valentine's

Day messages and suggest lunch meetings - not to discuss business but to maintain our personal connections.

How would it affect your sales if you had more relationships like that with your clients? If nothing else, it makes the hard work of being the high-performing professional you are a more enjoyable journey.

Making It Work for You

Networking really begins with enjoying meeting people and learning about them. So how do you start building a network? Building relationships? It's really simple: homework.

One of my success stories has been turning an office tower into a building full of clients. I started by looking at the Directory of Tenants in the lobby. (Check often, change happens quickly.) Research them: where is their main office? Where are decisions made?

The first client in the building started with nothing more than a hunch and curiosity. That's how I picked the name of the first company I was going to turn into a client. Then I started doing the real research on that company and its leaders: what the company did, its history, and who led the company. I searched through public records, associations, and every public source of information I could find, and I talked to everybody, including security. From that, I really started to know and like the people at that company before ever even meeting them.

I learned what we had in common - things like schools, hobbies, where our kids go to school, or charities we supported. Imagine how much easier starting a conversation is when you already know what interests the people you're talking with for the very first time! It makes asking the right questions very easy. It allowed me to find out who the decision maker would be.

My next step was visiting the client-to-be. I had a fantastic conversation with their receptionist, learned more about the company, and a lot about her. We eventually got around to business. When she asked how she could help me - and not the standard greeting for people walking in because we were way beyond that now - I was ready. I explained how I make my clients' lives better. Sure, I sell copiers, BUT I know how that makes hectic workdays easier and less costly.

I asked for her help in understanding how to get a meeting with the right person at her company. She helped me get that crucial meeting. Not right then, of course. She liked being the expert.

After a few more visits, the receptionist's help was crucial. She helped me know when to be there, who the key executive assistant was, and how to connect with her or him.

By the time I met with the key decision maker, I knew a lot about the families of that person, their assistant, and the receptionist. It made the sales conversation much easier and impactful. We ended up doing business. That was the first step in selling all the businesses in that office tower.

The next step was having an Open House at the client's offices to show off the new copiers and printers. I enjoyed doing events like that. When it doesn't work in their offices, then I use the lobby. That way, I get introduced to other key people at the businesses in the building. Then I repeat my research or "homework" for the next sale. And have another "Open House." This expands my network with every sale, plus I make a lot more friends.

While doing this, I also explain what supplies my growing client base can share when they have an emergency shortage. And eventually, there's an emergency of some kind. Knowing who you can call to get immediate toner replacement because your re-order was delayed by a snowstorm (which is a frequent winter challenge on the East Coast!) - or who uses the same specialty paper - can come in handy. Have you ever run out of toner or paper or staples when preparing a presentation late at night?

Repeating this relationship-building process has allowed me to convert multiple office towers and business "campuses" into clients. As people changed jobs and companies, they brought me along with them. My network of relationships continues to grow my network of clients.

Conclusion

The essence of successful networking isn't about techniques or tactics - it's about genuine human connection. When you focus on building real relationships rather than hunting for quick sales, you create a foundation for long-term success that benefits everyone involved.

Sure, sometimes you need a sale to make quotas or even this month's car payment. Your network of relationships - should you choose to build it - makes it possible to ask for help with finding the person or company needing your services TODAY. I have even called a client or two when I needed to win a contest, make a quota, and had a legit way to help them. I sent the paperwork right over, and they signed it for me even after business hours.

Remember, networking isn't just about who you know - it's about who knows they can trust you. When you put the client first, treat everyone with respect, and go above and beyond while staying authentic, you create connections that last a lifetime. Remembering the small touches, their birthdays, and personal struggles, goes a long way because so few people do that in business today. I've found this to be super fun and fulfilling, too!

If you don't enjoy getting to know people, if you don't feel fulfilled when helping other people, you'll struggle with networking. It will limit your options and could be a sign you're in the wrong business.

However, if you want to implement these lessons in your own networking efforts, here are my practical tips:

1. **Never network from desperation**. Build relationships first, and the business will follow naturally. A strong relationship with yourself is needed first. Be clear about what your values are and stick to them.

2. **Keep detailed records of your client interactions**. I maintained an unbelievable CRM system - when anyone took over after me, they couldn't believe how much information they had to work with. That made taking vacations (going to masterminds and traveling with my son's sports teams) easier because I knew my clients would still get world-class service.

3. **Remember the personal touches**. Send handwritten thank-you notes. Remember birthdays. Make people feel special because they are special, just like you. Show you're paying attention to them and truly care. Go the extra mile.

4. **Be willing to invest your own time and resources in relationship building**. The returns will far exceed the investment. Never rely on "the Company" to take care of it. Within reason, reach into your own pocket to build client relationships. And invest in yourself - reading, education, masterminds, networking events...it's all about proximity.

5. **Always be truthful about challenges, but come prepared with solutions**. Clients care more about how you handle problems. Sure, if problems are constant, that will be an issue for your clients. What's worse would be telling clients it will be handled when it's not. Just let them know what you're doing to solve a problem, and then go do it. Like we say at Nordstrom, "under promise, over deliver".

As I've learned throughout my journey from model to business leader, when you focus on building genuine relationships rather than making sales, success follows naturally. The key is to remain authentic, care genuinely about others' success, and be willing to go the extra mile to support their goals. After all, in business and in life, it's not just about what you achieve - it's about the lives you touch along the way.

Jeffrey A. Wolfe went from garage band dreams to advising Fortune 100 companies and the U.S. Military—without playing the traditional networking game. As founder of Adventure CEO® Media, he's built a media empire by mastering authentic relationship building over schmoozy business cards and elevator pitches. He's delivered transformative keynotes to everyone from scrappy startups to corporate giants, proving that real connections trump fake networking every time. His guiding principle, "Continually Expanding Opportunities," isn't just a motto—it's how he's opened doors most people never knew existed.

CHAPTER 8

FROM GARAGE BANDS TO GLOBAL INFLUENCE: THE NETWORKING HACK THAT OPENS ELITE DOORS

"Don't worry, they'll wait. It's my plane."
This guy's a real-life knight—actually knighted by Queen Elizabeth II.

Caught in that thought, I almost missed his invitation to sit at his table.

The chairman of a major international corporation was inviting my four colleagues and me to have a private meeting with him, while his ride back to London idled on the runway waiting for him. We took our places at his table.

Then he looked to me to start...

How did I get here?

I never imagined life's journey would lead from joining an engineering school just to graduate early from high school to the moment Sir William and my team were waiting for me to speak. Not to mention being one of the people to sign off on the first drawings released for the Delta III launch system. It was surreal. And I knew exactly what to say!

ROCK BANDS AND JOB OFFERS: GOING OFF-SCRIPT GETS TO THE REAL TOPIC

Networking. Building relationships. My dad coached me on that for years. It took a long time to sink in. And it actually worked.

It helped land my first job after engineering school. While most of my classmates were interviewing with Silicon Valley companies, I was determined to stay in the Midwest, so I skipped those opportunities. Then Hughes Aircraft arrived from Los Angeles. After more than a decade of reading their (award-winning) *Hughescope* inserts in *Scientific American*, I was fascinated by the leading-edge technologies they worked with. Howard Hughes's mystique and reputation added to my curiosity. I knew I'd regret not at least showing up.

A surprising lesson came out of that interview conversation: building a relationship led to a job offer. It was NOT what I'd expected.

We had a conversation about why I'd chosen engineering school, which was to design affordable wireless mics for our garage band. So, we talked about bands, gigs, and what equipment we used. Turns out, my interviewer played in a band (and still does). Our discussion built a relationship, and the hiring manager discerned I had the mindset required for being on his team. This outweighed my less-than-stellar grades. Saying yes to that offer became an inflection point in my life—a new path, leading to my conversation with Sir William.

Expensive corporate "sales trainers" often promote networking practices that focus on processes and transactional steps, like going to events, getting as many business contacts as possible, then relentlessly spamming everyone with email and voicemail until they either buy from you or sue you for harassment.

My experience has been more consistent with Merriam-Webster's definition:

"net-wer-kin, noun. 1: the exchange of information or services among individuals, groups, or institutions. Specifically: the cultivation of productive relationships for employment or business."

It's about strategic deep-dive relationship-building. Sure, that will lead to building a network of influence over time, but that happens one solid relationship at a time.

BIKERS, DONUTS, AND BONDS: NETWORKING BEYOND THE BOARDROOM

Networking has affected my personal life in powerful ways. Having a deep friendship with my motorcycle insurance agent led to building relationships at a Harley-Davidson dealership. (He enjoyed introducing his clients to each other and riding with them.)

In those days, I was riding up to 50,000 miles per year. Recommended preventive maintenance was every 2,500 miles. That meant tune-ups as often as three times a month! And there was a lot of competition for service appointments.

Saturdays were first-come, first-served scheduling. Service-entrance doors, in the alley behind the dealership, opened at 8:00 a.m. If you got there at 7:30 a.m., you weren't getting service that day. Riders started lining up before 7:00 a.m. Being in the first seven meant I could be on the road by 9:00 a.m. So, I showed up at 6:30 a.m., and two people were already there! Let's call them Bob and Rob.

Bob asked if we wanted coffee or donuts. He was going to the donut shop around the corner. Rob suggested the last one there should be buying. I blurted out, "Really?" turning to face them both with my best gunslinger stance. We stood there glaring at each other—three bikers in a deserted Los Angeles alley. A classic B-movie moment. My horrible *High Plains Drifter* imitation—asking, "...do you want cream or sugar with your coffee?"—forced groans and chuckles from Bob and Rob. Since Rob had been first to line up, I asked Bob if he would help me carry the coffee and donuts.

We returned to cheers from a line of riders because we had two boxes of donuts: one for the riders and one for the dealership's service department. Two more riders were dispatched to get more coffee to wash down the donuts. After that, every Saturday became a game: the second to arrive buys the coffee and donuts! So, always bring enough cash for a round of coffee and donuts, including the dealership staff. It was so competitive that I arrived at 5:00 a.m. to find another rider already there!

At this point, you're likely wondering, "What does this have to do with networking?"

I enjoyed meeting people. Those Saturdays included everyone from old-school bikers to successful entrepreneurs to A-list actors. We talked about our bikes, favorite roads, and life. Being one of the few who bought extra donuts, especially for the service department, I got lots of attention. One of the mechanics invited me to their Sunday rides through Southern California's mountains.

I was experiencing what my dad taught me many years before about building relationships, and my life became more fun as a result. Business networking became enjoyable instead of a necessary evil type of task.

TURNING CHAOS INTO TRIUMPH: 360-DEGREE RELATIONSHIP-BUILDING

My professional career reflected this. I earned a management position on a team turning around a troubled product launch at an aviation electronics company.

There were six of us. The contract was for over $100,000,000. Our customer was very angry, and sent attorneys because we were behind schedule. Our mission was to get deliveries on schedule while transitioning from the design/development phase into the production phase. (Imagine trying to build cars while engineering changes were still flying in like an East Coast drone swarm!) Every day started with a 7:00 a.m. standing meeting—no chairs—20 minutes, six managers, three minutes to update scheduled tasks, declare risks, ask for any help needed.

Experiences like the Saturday motorcycle maintenance gatherings gave me an edge. I had become comfortable building relationships with a wide range of personalities, including lots of banter and taunts. That honed an ability to get through heated management meetings without piling up resentments toward other managers who attacked my team as a strategy for defending theirs.

I strategically built relationships with the network of people needed as allies to get the job at hand done. And not just "management." Several key allies worked on the production line. "Management" had earned a reputation for looking down their noses at production team members. I took an interest in their problems—business and personal. Some of those relationships stayed very transactional, some became deep friendships. BUT I earned their respect and trust surprisingly quickly.

Being curious, genuinely caring, and asking the right questions made it all possible.

I repeated that with other managers who had been openly hostile to my predecessor. Instead of battling each other, we began collaborating.

It was truly 360-degree networking across the org chart. And it worked. Our department performed better than it had in years. All departments banding together made it possible to turn a hostile customer into a very happy one.

SCALING SUCCESS: FROM SMALL WINS TO MILLION-DOLLAR DEALS

Years later, working for a consulting firm, these networking skills became even more crucial. The firm provided engineering and training services to small manufacturing companies (less than 500 employees). Our goal was to increase revenue per client engagement.

Using what I'd learned from building corporate-level teams, I started getting to know the consultants. That required making staff meetings and company events non-negotiable on my calendar. Many of our consultants only grudgingly attended when forced to, but I knew doing this strategically would pay off.

Building a network of relationships made it possible to rapidly assemble teams to deliver larger projects for clients. When I proposed a project ten times our average contract, some claimed it was impossible to sell. After selling it, a few said we couldn't deliver, but I already had those who wanted to deliver on the project team. Our client got more than a 3:1 return on their investment before we finished the work. Over the next 18 months, we increased the company's average contract size by a factor of ten.

WHEN NETWORKING FAILS: EMBRACING THE STING OF SETBACKS

Let's face it, not every networking effort or opportunity will yield the desired results. For example, I participated in a Saturday breakfast club for three years, twice a month. Over 100 business leaders attended, most in my target market. I even helped with media production and bringing in guest speakers. But I had to admit there would never be anything more than superficial acquaintances in that group.

While I did connect with some of the speakers and had them as guests on my podcast series, nothing else seemed likely. On paper, it looked like an ideal networking opportunity. The reality proved it was not. Admitting that stung. FOMO (Fear of Missing Out) hit hard when I didn't renew my membership. That was a great group, just not on my path. It was a stinging reminder that true social networking must be based on things I'm passionate about and enjoy doing. Networking at business events tends to be more focused.

For every great networking success I've experienced, there have been several that didn't pan out. It's not about numbers—that's a transactional mindset. It's about enjoying the journey. Networking opportunities I didn't enjoy never yielded good results. Even enjoying the process doesn't guarantee success, either. BUT I was having fun every time I made a great networking connection!

Do you enjoy "networking?" What is your expectation when "networking?"

Everything changed for me with this mindset shift: everyone I meet will either teach me something that will help me achieve my goals, they will refer me to a crucial "contact," or they will become a client. One meaningful connection at each networking opportunity can create massive success.

FROM LUNCH TO JAPAN: THE POWER OF ONLINE CONNECTIONS

Networking doesn't just happen face-to-face. My social media network created an extraordinary speaking opportunity—in Japan—for a colleague. We were catching up over lunch when I asked him what would be most helpful for him. He joked, "Who do you know in Japan?" He was traveling to Japan for vacation with his partner. "A speaking gig there would mean I'm officially an international speaker! Thus, expanding my business outside the USA."

"Let me look into that," I responded. I had loosely kept in touch with a colleague who had returned home to Japan. The next step created astounding results! Simply sending greetings and a request for their "advice and counsel" resulted in a new connection in Japan. The person I was referred to researched my American colleague's website. An excited call to a professional group he was a member of resulted in more than an offer to speak. They created a special event that fit my American colleague's travel schedule. The pictures from his first international speaking engagement reflected high energy in a packed room.

"Let me look into that" has become an inside joke between us. And his promotional materials now say International Speaker.

THE BIRTHDAY TEXT THAT MEANT EVERYTHING: SIMPLE WAYS TO MAINTAIN REAL CONNECTIONS

Maintaining networks poses a growing challenge. The more people you know, the more work it takes. Social media helps with this. Birthdates are often shared, making it easy to send a "Happy Birthday!" Just that simple act has an impact.

A colleague going through a tough year responded with a heartfelt thank you. I had been one of the very few to reach out that year, and it made an outsized difference.

You likely know at least one person who only emails or messages when they want something. Do you want to make other people feel the way you do when getting that message? I had a very well-known "marketing guru" email and call more than ten times a day after I requested a free guide they offered. I'll never buy from or recommend that person. I still cringe every time I hear that person's name.

However, an occasional book or podcast recommendation builds more trust. And by occasional, I mean weekly at most. Since so few people send cards via regular mail, an annual birthday card gets noticed more than ever. I strive to send a personal "Happy Birthday" to all my Facebook friends. There are rarely more than ten a day, which only takes a few minutes. However, there are ways to delegate and/or automate follow-ups going out regularly.

SAVING AN INDUSTRY: NETWORKING ON A NATIONAL STAGE

Imagine being asked to help save an entire industry. That's a challenge I accepted from the National Institute of Standards and Technology (NIST).

Part of the "Peace Dividend" after the end of the Cold War in the early 1990s was the consolidation of the Aerospace & Defense Industry. In less than a decade, the 136 prime contractors supplying the Department of Defense (DoD) decreased to nine. Imagine the impact on the supply chain! How would losing 93% of your customers affect your business?

National security concerns over losing chunks of that supply chain drove the search for ways to preserve it. Smaller, mostly family-owned manufacturing companies that had supported the DoD since World War II were at greatest risk. Many had difficult, sometimes impossible-to-recreate skills.

A massive networking effort was needed. Of the nine remaining DoD contractors, I networked into the corporate leadership of six. A U.S. Air Force officer was my point of contact with the DoD. Several NIST-sponsored organizations across the USA needed to be brought into the effort, as well as technical experts. Members of Congress needed to be part of this, since they ultimately controlled the purse strings. Then, state-level politicians, too.

Yet, the process was quite simple. First, I had to answer two questions:

1. Who do we need on board to advance our efforts? And who do we need on board to avoid being vetoed?
2. How do we identify the companies to help?

There were still over two million people working in the industry, after more than one million had been fired. That meant thousands of businesses to potentially help. Not all of those would survive, no matter what we did. But which were truly critical to the supply chain?

Answering that question gets beyond our discussion here. I can say this: the network of allies developed at DoD, NIST, the prime contractors, and the Aerospace Industries Association (AIA) provided the insights for our best possible answer at that time.

Networking was also needed for the "who" question. We mapped out individuals by company and position, then researched who held those positions. We mapped out the chain of people that would connect us to those people. Then we combined our connections to get meetings. It took time and travel.

The result was several million dollars in funding for the projects to transition manufacturing companies from military contracts to commercial-use production. We created a model that was deployed nationally, while continually incorporating lessons learned.

A SEAT AT THE KNIGHT'S ROUNDTABLE: THE POWER OF NETWORKING

Sir William (his name has been changed to protect his privacy) was the closing keynote speaker at an aerospace-industry conference. It was a lunch session. There were maybe 200 people in the room, mostly industry VIPs.

Seated at our table was the corporate-level team I'd built at a Fortune 500 company. That team contributed to changing how products are developed by integrating new technologies. The team included one representative from each major business unit, incorporating proven best practices into our company processes. We were risking our careers by leading changes that affected over 65,000 employees. Truly, it was a merry band of brothers.

A greeting line filled with industry VIPs formed as soon as Sir William finished his speech. Wrapping around the room, they looked like a stalled conga line waiting for music. I got up and took my place in line.

My colleagues were stunned. "We can't talk to him, he's the CHAIRMAN," hissed one of the team members. Chuckling, I quickly responded, "Look, they'll let us know if they don't want us in the line." One of the more mischievous team members shrugged, grinned, and jumped in line. And we were off.

All standing there after three exhausting days of travel and meetings, the waiting began. And continued. It seemed like an eternity—all 30 minutes of it.

We were finally next in line. But a C-suite member of a Fortune 500 company asked if he could jump the line because his plane's takeoff time was imminent. "Of course!" I smiled. He paused long enough to read our ID badges, nodded thanks, then turned to speak with Sir William.

We were next! Until a U.S. Military General with multiple stars on his shoulders and a chest full of ribbons and medals asked if HE could step in front of us. "Of course!" I smiled.

"Thank you, Son. Excellent VR presentation." (I had led the first Virtual Reality Uses breakout session for that group a year earlier.) He read our ID badges, then turned to speak to Sir William.

Sweating, my feet hurting, so tired I felt dizzy, I turned and smiled at my team. "We're next!"

The General turned, nodded to us, and marched off.

As Sir William greeted our team, a very large man with a coiled wire dangling from his ear walked up behind our soon-to-be host, stating, "Sir, we need to go. The plane's ready for takeoff."

All that waiting for nothing!

Sir William smiled as he said, "Thank you. Don't worry, they'll wait. It's my plane. They can't take off without me."

Stunned, mouths hanging open, we looked at each other.

Gesturing to us, Sir William said, "These gentlemen have been waiting so patiently. Please sit with me. We've all been standing so long. Let an old man rest."

Speechless, we sat—the five of us and Sir William. A tall, executive-looking man stood at Sir William's right shoulder. Sir William asked us to introduce ourselves and tell him our roles at the company. Then everyone looked at me and waited.

"How did I get here?" echoed in my head.

Fortunately, I had a question prepared for him. After thanking him for being so gracious with his time, I asked the question. The actual question wouldn't be as relevant to our discussion here as my key insight from that conversation: Always thank the speaker, and be prepared to graciously ask ONE brief, relevant question.

After answering my question, Sir William paid us all a huge compliment that added confidence to our career trajectories. After another reminder that the plane was powered up and waiting, our time with Sir William came to an end.

Then the executive standing at his right shoulder walked over to me. Shaking my hand, looking me straight in the eye, he pulled out a business card. "Pleasure to meet you. Next time you're in town, call me. I'd love to give you a plant tour! Lunch is on me."

I thanked him as he handed me the card. He and Sir William, along with their security entourage, walked out the door. I looked at his card. "President" leapt out at me—as in president of their U.S.A. operations.

Did it take me 45 minutes to get a corporate president to invite me to his company for lunch, or years of networking effort? Perhaps both.

The key to it all was being curious, taking action, and enjoying the journey.

YOUR PATH TO MORE INFLUENCE: FIVE STEPS TO TRANSFORM YOUR NETWORKING GAME

My experience has been that networking is about relationships. It's so simple, I missed it for years.

Would you mind if I offered something for your consideration, based on those years of experience? Taking action on five simple steps changed everything for me. One or more will likely accelerate your journey, too:

1. **Be genuinely curious about people.** If you don't like people and don't find them interesting...don't network.

2. **Look for common interests and ways to be helpful.** Karma works; make it positive. My experience has been that it feels good to do the right thing and be of service where possible. And people appreciate it; they reciprocate.

3. **Be strategic.** Know who you know, and who they know. Then do your homework on people you need to cultivate as allies. Have you ever played "6 Degrees of Kevin Bacon?" It's based on the theory that any two people are no more than six connections apart. I'm one person from Kevin Bacon and two from the President of the United States. You're likely closer than you realize!

4. **Be prepared.** Know what you want to ask. Be brief, relevant, and gracious. Most people appreciate that because too many of those approaching them are neither. High performers relish sharing their wisdom, helping others along their journey. And DO NOT attempt any kind of pitch or sale!

5. **Enjoy the journey!** If you're not having fun, stop. You're either doing it wrong or in the wrong business. Not every networking opportunity will be convenient or a place you really want to be. I've found there's something or someone

entertaining about nearly all of them, making for enjoyable experiences.

YOUR FUTURE AWAITS: A CHALLENGE TO CONNECTWITHTHEALLEGEDLYUNREACHABLE

Here's a challenge, should you choose to accept it: Name somebody you really admire but feel there's no way you could get access to.

Then:

1. Research what their likes/dislikes and pet projects are.
2. Create a powerful question you'd like to ask for their advice and counsel on.
3. Map out the chain of relationships that could get you to that person.
4. Work that chain of relationships to get in touch with the person you've named.
5. Get your question answered either face-to-face or in writing.
6. Mail a thank-you card within 24 hours.

Six simple actions!

When you've completed the challenge, I'd like to hear what you learned along the way.

If you'd like to brainstorm ideas for completing the challenge, I'll gladly volunteer 30 minutes to talk with you.

I'm looking forward to hearing your successes and learnings! Reach out to me at LetsTalk@AdventureCEO.com.

Robert Commodari comes from a family of seven siblings, growing up in Northeast Baltimore City. He started working at eleven and paid his way through private high school and college.

In 1990, he read his first inspirational book, and over the last 34 years, he has read over 1,200 books.

Rob is a passionate speaker, a #1 bestselling author of *Better Than You Think*, a co-author of the #1 bestseller *Next Level Your Life*, and host of the podcast *Chiseled*. He's spoken to thousands of people over the years, inspiring them to develop awareness to live a more fulfilling life. Rob leads his own real estate group and has sold over 2000 homes in his 24-year career.

CHAPTER 9
Learning to Play in the Right Sandbox

Robert Commodari grew up in Northeast Baltimore City as one of seven siblings. He started working at eleven and paid his way through private high school and college. In 1990, he read his first inspirational book, and over the last 34 years, he has read more than twelve hundred books. Rob is a passionate speaker, a #1 bestselling author of *Better Than You Think*, a co-author of the #1 bestseller *Next Level Your Life*, and host of the podcast *Chiseled*. He's spoken to thousands of people across the country.

Rob has been in the real estate business for over 23 years now and leads a four-person team averaging approximately 100 transactions per year. In 2021, The Commodari Group closed 130 transactions. Rob works primarily by referral and believes that by working by referral, you build deeper relationships along the way, which in turn helps develop a lifelong business.

I've been a part of several network communities over the years for purposes of life, work, and spirituality. Networking isn't about going to a conference and handing out business cards, telling everyone you "networked." Networking is about connecting with people and building relationships with them. It's about building and gaining trust. You have to be trusted to receive connections from others, and you also have to be a trusted person so that others can trust the people you connect with.

The reader will learn from this chapter the importance of building networks in different areas of life. It could be a spiritual network, a business network, a financial network, a network of dancers, etc. It's about building and belonging to communities in a networking sense. Years ago, I participated in a Memory Ball for Alzheimer's and raised $70,000. I was so tunnel-visioned, I only thought of networks in a business sense. What I learned was that there is a network for everything. I was introduced to a community (network) of people who focused on ballroom dancing. Then, when I tapped into my business network of Realtors and other business people, I made connections with people who I didn't know had an interest in ballroom dancing, and I learned of so many clients and people who were—and are currently—connected to Alzheimer's, either personally or from a charitable standpoint.

I got into the real estate business in 2001 at the age of 33. At the time, I had a newspaper business in Baltimore City. I had 16 people working for me, and I would get up every morning at 1:30 a.m. to meet those who worked for me and/or deliver newspapers myself. While strolling the city streets for nine years, I noticed how houses were transforming in front of my eyes—from dilapidated homes into renovated gems. There was a consistency of real estate signs on houses, so I got to know who the popular agents were. That led me to gain an interest in becoming a Realtor.

I grew up thinking I had to spend money to make money. I think the quote should have been, "You have to spend money wisely or strategically to make money." My first year in the real estate business, I grossed $41,000 in business but netted $1,000. That's it?! Then one day, while walking into a real estate office, I saw a flyer from a coaching and training company on coaching agents on how to do business by referral. The only reason I had interest in the moment was because he had an Italian last name, as did I. A silly reason to think that way, but certainly the truth. The name of the coaching company at that time was Providence, owned and operated by Brian Buffini. The name of the company has since changed to Buffini and Company.

I signed up as a coaching client for Buffini and Company in 2002. It was then that I learned more about networking. I realized that if I was going to make this business work, especially by referral, I had to learn and understand the concept of networking. There are different areas of networking for the same business. By being in the Buffini community and attending his events (four or five a year), I learned there was value in networking with the agents at these events. In my limited thinking, I was under the impression that I had to know people in my geographic area, and I could only get business locally from family and friends and from other business people I knew. What I discovered was that there was an entirely different community to network with that would result in another source of income. Networking with agents across the country would generate hundreds of thousands of gross commission income over the last 20-plus years. This occurred in three ways: first, I would ask the agents if they had someone moving to Maryland; I would love to be the agent they refer business to. Secondly, if I had someone moving out of state, I could connect them with someone within the network of the Buffini community. And finally, it was possible that I might know someone out of state who was moving from one state to another that wouldn't involve me as their agent, but I could connect two agents together and generate a referral fee from both the buyer and seller sides.

Then there was the idea of connecting with family and friends at a deeper level, so they would have an understanding that I was in business as a Realtor, and I desired to be their trusted advisor in real estate. So, I had to network with family and friends to accomplish this. Finally, there was the idea of networking with business people to generate referrals from their networks. I would begin going to small meetings with business owners or salespeople to build deeper relationships to become a trusted advisor for them. For lack of a better word, I was running for mayor to get their vote or gain their trust.

Time, money, and my own insecurities were challenges that I would face. First, I had to work the business, and the busier I got, the more my time was challenged. So I had to learn to prioritize my time to determine what meetings or events were worth attending and which ones might not be the best use of my time. Concerning the financial challenge, it was an investment of money to be a part of the coaching community. Then there was the expense of traveling to the events. Flights, hotels, and meals were an investment. Was it worth the return? Of course! It's easy to say in hindsight, but when you're young and beginning your career, you must watch where you invest your money. I had to have faith in the systems and in myself. Which brings me to the third challenge I mentioned: my own insecurities. Often in life, I've questioned my self-worth. I would go through what they call Imposter Syndrome. Was I good enough, smart enough, or who would want to do business with me? Those were the questions I would ask myself. Especially growing up as an introvert, I was beginning a business in which I knew I would have to become more of an extrovert to succeed at a high level. Some might argue that.

THE JOURNEY

The journey has been incredible—not just in real estate, but in personal development as well. I have written a book, launched a podcast, and become a sought-after speaker. Each of these steps required learning to connect with people in new ways.

I attended real estate events, but also seminars on podcasting, writing, and speaking. I joined Toastmasters to improve my communication skills—an investment that made me not just a better speaker, but a better listener.

Through it all, the Buffini Community remained the epicenter of my growth. It fueled my business, but more importantly, it introduced me to lifelong friends, mentors, and opportunities. Through that community, I met real estate agents across the country and forged relationships with many of Buffini's guest speakers—relationships that continue to impact my life today.

Buffini didn't just teach networking and sales; he taught personal growth and development, and that made all the difference.

HAVE A STORY

A breakthrough moment came for me in 2002 at a Buffini Conference. During the event, Brian Buffini shared some of his family background—he was one of six siblings, raised in a 710-square-foot house with just two bedrooms and one bathroom. I immediately related. I'm one of seven, and we grew up in a 745-square-foot home. Though Brian was born in Ireland and I was raised in Baltimore, we shared a connection through our Italian heritage—my father was born in Italy.

Feeling moved, I wrote Brian a letter sharing my own family history and a deeply personal story: my first game of catch with my father, at age 34.

My dad worked three jobs to keep our family afloat. Like many men of his generation, he wasn't one to express emotion. I had never heard him say, "I love you." He gave me my first baseball glove—a hand-me-down—when I was five. Baseball became my passion, but we never played catch.

Years later, after Cal Ripken Sr.'s death made headlines, I started reflecting on the relationship between fathers and sons. I realized that I had never had that classic moment of connection with my dad. I set out to find that original glove and ask him to play catch with me for Christmas. After five months of searching, I found the glove buried beneath a heavy box in a closet—just five days before Christmas. The only reason I found the glove was that my dad needed to get something out of the box that had to be removed from the closet to find what he was looking for. He had recently had surgery and wasn't able to lift anything heavy. When I lifted the box and turned to pull it out of the closet, to my shock and surprise, the glove was lying under the box. Who knows how many years the glove had been lying there, but it was certainly a providential and emotional moment for sure!

On Christmas Day, 2001, we went outside, and my mom took a photo of us playing catch. For me, it was more than a game—it was a healing moment. According to Gary Chapman's *The Five Love Languages*, mine is "words of affirmation," and I had never heard "I love you" or "I accept you" from my dad.

But that day, when I tossed him the ball and he caught it, I heard, in my heart, "I accept you, son." And when he threw it back to me, I heard, "I love you." That emotional exchange helped me release years of striving and self-doubt. It was like taking my foot off the brake of my life.

Shortly after sending the letter to Brian, he began sharing the story at his events. Thousands heard it. One agent, moved by the story, approached me afterward and offered a referral for a client moving from Oregon to Baltimore City—a deal that earned me over $25,000.

Over the next three years, Brian shared the story across the country. Agents remembered me and began sending referrals.

Did I get lucky? Maybe. Was it divine intervention? Absolutely! I believe the hand of Providence was at work. That one authentic moment opened the doors to hundreds of relationships and significant business growth.

BUILDING THE NETWORK

Over the years, I've met some extraordinary people through Buffini events. One example was Bob Beaudine—dubbed by *Sports Illustrated* as "the most influential man in sports you've never heard of." After reading his books, *The Power of Who* and *Two Chairs*, I reached out and thanked him. We spoke a few times, and within a week, I interviewed him on my podcast *Chiseled*. We've since developed a strong friendship.

My desire to speak professionally has been years in the making, and my background in personal development spans more than three decades. A few Mastermind friends encouraged me to connect with Kyle Wilson, Jim Rohn's longtime business partner and founder of Jim Rohn International. I hadn't heard of Kyle before, but after being introduced through Ben Andrews, whom I met in the Buffini community, I joined a collaborative book project led by Kyle.

That connection led to more. I joined Kyle's Inner Circle Group, attending events at his home in Dallas and online. Kyle gave me a chance to speak at one of his events—despite never having heard me speak before. It went so well that he introduced me to NBA championship coach Kevin Eastman and two-time U.S. Memory Champion Ron White. In 2024, I presented with both of them in Baltimore on two separate occasions.

Soon after, I was invited to a Mastermind at the home of personal growth legend Dennis Waitley. I've since developed a friendship with Dennis as well.

From there, I was introduced to Ken Walls, host of *Breakthrough Walls*, one of the top-ranked podcasts. Ken then connected me with influential leaders like Paul Hutchinson, Jeffrey Gitomer, James Keyes, and Mark Victor Hansen. Many of them became guests on *Chiseled*, where I had the privilege of learning from their stories—and building friendships with them along the way.

Through this journey, I've earned millions in real estate, but more importantly, I've become a better communicator and listener. I've learned to lead with curiosity and to stay rooted in personal growth. Attending events led me to other speakers, authors, and thought leaders I wouldn't have otherwise met. These relationships deepened my understanding of what makes people successful—and how they think.

The System

The Buffini system is a simple yet powerful approach to building relationships—focused on contact, care, and community.

It starts with making contact. That means using an age-old tool: the phone. We also reach out via Zoom, email, and even through the mail. However, there's nothing like voice-to-voice or face-to-face contact to build real trust. In today's tech-driven world, people text more than they talk. That's convenient—but it doesn't build depth.

Next is care. We show people we care by investing our most valuable resource—our time. Visiting people at home or their workplace deepens the relationship in a way digital tools never can. A small side note: never show up empty-handed. Years ago, my wife Debbie suggested I bring a bottle of ketchup when visiting clients—just to let them know I was stopping by to "ketch-up." It's corny, but it always brings a smile.

And finally, we build community. This could be client appreciation parties or business events within your database. I've done this consistently for almost two decades, but there's always room to grow. Mastering this in real estate taught me I could apply the same system to podcasting and speaking.

Some people are results-driven, and they may find this process too slow. But I've learned you can't control the results—you can only control your activities. If I want to increase my numbers, I either have to do more of the right activities or get better at the ones I'm already doing. The system works—but it requires time, intention, and consistency.

Content and Lifelong Lessons

Being part of these networks has done more than expand my reach—it's shaped me personally and professionally. Over the years, I've developed countless friendships, some surface-level, many deep and lasting. Beyond the relationships, the content shared and the lessons learned have been priceless.

At Brian Buffini's Peak Experience seminars, especially the first three, I experienced profound personal growth. At the first event, I learned what it meant to be transparent. For years, I believed I had to wear a tough exterior, avoiding vulnerability. But I discovered that transparency is not weakness—it's attractive, liberating, and life-changing. It was like being handed a "Get Out of Jail Free" card for my emotions.

At the second Peak Experience, Brian introduced the concept of Contemplative Prayer. I didn't just hear it—I leaned into it. For six consecutive years, I practiced it regularly. That single spiritual discipline sparked another surge in my growth.

At the third event, Brian brought in Joe Erhmann, a former NFL player for the Baltimore Colts. Joe spoke on "Learning How to Love and Be Loved"—a concept that hit home. He also revealed the three lies society tells young men and women that prevent us from becoming who we were truly created to be. That message stuck with me.

These experiences—along with countless others—are why I credit so much of my growth to the Buffini Community.

One of the most pivotal moments came when I met Curtis Oaks at a Buffini event. One day, out of the blue, he called and said, "Something told me to tell you—you'll go to the next level in your life and business when you trust that voice inside." That message changed me. I began to tune in to that inner voice— what I believe is the Holy Spirit—and learned to trust it. That voice guided me through major decisions, including writing my book *Better Than You Think* and launching my podcast *Chiseled*, which now has over 100 episodes. The craziest of all was going to jail, I guess (lol), to inspire the inmates to have hope. The voice was telling me to title my speech in prison *Jailbreak*. It was a huge success, and it made a major impact on the inmates.

As you've read, the relationships and business I've built through networking have been incredible. I've sold over 2,000 homes, most through referral, and generated millions in commissions. That didn't happen by luck—it happened by earning trust and showing up with intention.

Now, I plan to use the same system to grow my speaking and mentoring platforms.

It's all about choosing the sandbox you want to play in. Define your purpose—personally and professionally—and identify the people and networks that align with it. Bring value. Ask questions. Be authentic. When you operate from that place, people are drawn to you. You'll be invited into new rooms, new relationships, and your network will expand—at whatever pace and depth you desire.

Consistency is key. Depth is everything.

Be a giver, not a taker. Too many people approach networking to see what they can get. The truth is, the most powerful growth comes when you focus on giving. As Brian Buffini says, "Give it out in slices, and it will come back in loaves."

Jessica Lund is from a small town in central Utah called Manti. She is a member of the Church of Jesus Christ of Latter-day Saints. She holds a Master's Degree in Health and Wellness Coaching from Creighton University and is a National Board Certified Health and Wellness Coach. She loves spending time with her husband and family. She teaches at a local community college, where her favorite class to teach every semester is called Dealing with Life. She enjoys helping people make changes and learn about their bodies so that they can live a happier and healthier life.

Instagram: @jessicalund.ms

CHAPTER 10
Growing Your Support System

It was September 22, 2021, and I had just been hired as a career advisor at a community college. My supervisor, Lisa, and I were setting up a job fair for students searching for employment throughout the school year. It was one of the first events I was heading up in my new position, and I was excited. My brother called to inform me that my dad had just tested positive for COVID-19. We had been to dinner with him the night before and knew that we both needed to be tested.

Since he was a student and I was an employee at the college, we could be tested on campus. Both of us were apprehensive as we waited for our results. It only took about two minutes before the employee administering the test told us that we were both positive and needed to leave campus to quarantine. Disappointed, I called Lisa to apologize for not being able to return or help carry out one of our biggest events of the semester.

While I was positive with COVID, I was mildly sick. I had a slight fever, a light cough, and some nausea. I lost my taste and smell for less than a day. It wasn't a big deal for me. Little did I know, four months later, my whole life would change. I would develop Long COVID, and it would be so much worse than COVID itself had been. Many symptoms of Long COVID can be similar from person to person. However, it is also true that Long COVID can affect everyone differently. For me, being a long-hauler came with many symptoms. Some of them were common: brain fog, fatigue, headaches, and shortness of breath, but one, called parosmia, was fairly unique.

January 6, 2022, started as a normal day. My husband, Jayden, and I were traveling to Las Vegas, NV, after work. I was eating a salad for lunch and decided to call him to talk about a few of our plans. While I was on the phone with him, I bit into a piece of spinach. It did not taste good. I tried another piece and then told Jayden that I didn't like spinach anymore. I didn't think too much about this discovery, since having COVID, some foods occasionally tasted a bit strange.

After work, I met Jayden at home. We finished packing and began the long drive to Las Vegas. On the way, he stopped for a late lunch of chicken strips and fries. As soon as the food was within smelling distance, I knew something was off. I decided to investigate by tearing a chicken strip open, smelling, and tasting it. As soon as I had taken a bite, I immediately spit it out because the taste was overwhelmingly rotten. Jayden didn't seem to notice anything wrong with it and continued eating. We wrote off my experience and decided that chicken must just be another food that tasted wrong due to COVID.

About five hours later, we pulled into Las Vegas and decided to get dinner after checking into our hotel. As we walked through the casino, I noticed another weird smell. When we sat down for dinner, I began to understand that something was really wrong with me. Everything around me smelled terrible. We ordered a few types of food in hopes that I could find something to eat. I ended up pulling the cheese off a piece of pizza and eating a few croutons.

The next day was much worse. We walked past a pizza place in a food court, and I smelled the worst smell of my life. I had to ask what it was. Jayden told me it was the pizza. I could no longer differentiate or recognize any smells. I needed to find a solution to my new problem as quickly as possible. This led me to search the internet for anyone who could help, remedies to try, and a support group with people who understood how instantly life-altering this condition was.

With parosmia, your desire to eat, attend social events, or be around anyone who has used a fragrant personal care product severely decreases. Making plans is extremely difficult when you don't know what food will be close by or what smells you may encounter. Your quality of life significantly decreases when everything tastes and/or smells like sewage, decomposition, or rotting meat. You constantly feel that you are missing out on life.

The first full day dealing with parosmia left me full of anxiety. What would I eat now? How long would this last? Why did it settle into my body so quickly? Would anyone believe that this was actually real and not just in my head? Were there other people dealing with this? If so, how many? Would any doctor be able to help me navigate a treatment plan? Was there even a treatment plan formulated? Or was COVID still so new that nobody would have any idea about what might help? Would this be permanent? How many social gatherings or holidays with family and friends would I have to miss because being around food made me sick to my stomach? What kind of strain would this put on my relationships? How sick was this actually going to make me?

During our trip, we visited multiple buffets so that I could try a variety of foods and figure out what I could tolerate and what I needed to avoid. By the time we left Las Vegas, I figured that I could eat sourdough and some white breads (but not if there was too much yeast in them), some dairy (white cheeses were easiest and yogurt had to be unflavored), tomatoes (which had always been my least favorite vegetable), pasta with butter, most vanilla flavored desserts (if they were made with real vanilla), and Dr. Pepper. Having studied nutrition as an undergrad, I knew that this was possibly the least ideal diet that a person could eat. I would need to supplement almost everything if I were to remain somewhat healthy.

During the drive home, I decided to begin navigating the steep learning curve of finding a network of people who also dealt with this challenge. It turns out that there was a fast-growing Facebook group specifically for people with parosmia. Everyone was sharing their "safe foods" and different remedies they had tried. I spent hours reading posts in this group, hoping to find anything that might help. It was interesting to read different posts by people saying that their spouse or their families didn't believe that what they were experiencing was real. I am lucky enough to have a husband who is so supportive and willing to let me try anything and everything to fix OUR problem. He constantly reminds me that we're in this life together, and we are going to deal with whatever comes our way together. There are not enough words that I can say or write to express how grateful I am for him. Parosmia forced us into a new community, and we have now been privileged enough to meet some truly wonderful people throughout the country because of it.

One night, I was scrolling through the new posts on Facebook. There was a CRNA in Texas who was offering help to people with Parosmia. He explained that a procedure he was doing was helping long-haulers. The procedure is called a Stellate Ganglion Block (SBG). Basically, an SGB is an injection of local anesthetic, guided by ultrasound, into both sides of your neck near your voice box. The idea is that it resets your nervous system and pulls you out of a fight-or-flight state. He explained that it was mostly used for pain management and PTSD, but it was showing promising results for patients with parosmia. Being in Utah, traveling to Texas for a procedure seemed a little crazy to me. However, I knew there was a pain clinic in a town about 15 miles away that might offer this treatment. I knew the NP who worked at this clinic and immediately sent her a message explaining my situation, his findings, and asked if she thought her office could help. Within a matter of days, I was at a consultation discussing the procedure. During the consult, I was made to feel completely crazy as I was told, "People don't just forget how to taste, smell, or eat." After hearing this, I was devastated but decided to go through with the procedure anyway. It did not work as well as I had hoped; however, it did give me more hope that my parosmia would eventually go away. Because of the way I was treated at this clinic, I also began looking for another clinic that could perform the procedure, one that would believe that my experience was real and not just in my head.

I continued to chat with people online who were dealing with parosmia. By this time, April 2022, I had been living this nightmare for four months. I learned that there was another office, about an hour and a half away, that could perform the same procedure. I wanted to try it again because so many people were finding relief. The second office was wonderful to work with. They didn't have anyone on-site who could do the SGB, but they knew that many people were suffering from Long COVID, so they were flying a doctor in from their sister clinic in San Diego to try to help. This office felt so much more caring and understood the potentially promising effects of the SGB. Before administering the blocks, Dr. Michael Ming asked me a variety of questions, including, "How is your support system?" He went on to explain how he had seen families torn apart because of parosmia. I explained to him that my husband and family were the best in the world, and each of them would do anything and everything they could to help me. He reinforced just how lucky I was, because that wasn't the case for many of his patients. After this round of SGBs, I had a few good days. Then things went backward. Because I had made some progress, it felt like everything was taken away from me, for a second time. It is extremely hard and depressing when anyone goes through an experience that feels like a setback. I was so nervous to keep seeking treatment, but I knew that I couldn't continue to live this way forever.

In October 2022, I finally mustered the courage to do another round of SGBs. This time, after the procedure, I was normal! It was a miracle. I ate an apple and began to cry because it was the first time in 10 months that I had eaten a piece of fruit. Life was wonderful... until I started to regress again. I had three great days, and then the horrible tastes and smells came back with a vengeance. I was worse than I had ever been.

I continued to learn more about the condition and the different treatments that people were trying. I found a Long COVID clinical trial for anosmia (loss of taste and smell) being done at Jefferson University in Philadelphia. Since I had some sensation of taste and smell, and I had done multiple SGBs, I didn't qualify for the trial. However, the woman I spoke with on the phone let me know that they were seeing promising results, and this treatment would likely be offered to the public in the spring. She took my name and said she would check back in with me once the trial had ended. The next February, 13 months into my parosmia journey, I received a phone call from her and scheduled a series of appointments. In March, Jayden and I were on a plane to Philadelphia. This office was performing a platelet-rich plasma (PRP) treatment. It consisted of drawing my blood, spinning it down to the PRP, dipping a biodegradable sponge in it, and then sticking the sponge up my nose, where it would settle in behind my eyes. The goal was that the PRP would help correct any olfactory nerve damage that COVID may have caused. This treatment had helped patients whose sense of taste and smell had not returned since contracting COVID, but parosmia was a whole different ballgame. Hearing this was challenging, but Dr. David Rosen gave me some hope when he said, "This is a problem that your body is having. It has to eventually figure it out because you cannot live this way forever." We visited Philadelphia three times in three months for this treatment. There were minor changes that we tracked via a smell test that was given before the procedure. During my first appointment, I was able to guess two out of 12 smells correctly. By the end of the treatment series, I was able to guess five of them. This meant that I had improved by three smells, but it still left me with a failing score. Without completing the smell tests, I don't think that I could have noticed that any progress had been made. I was still hopeful, thanks to Dr. Rosen's confidence that my body would learn to be normal again.

But I was back to square one, again. Since we had been trying to fix my nerves to no avail, I decided that I wanted to try focusing on my brain instead. The next month, I was back on a plane heading to California to the Amen Clinics to meet with more doctors, have my brain scanned, start a new treatment plan, and hopefully find some answers. While I was scheduling my visit, I was told that no one knew if this would help treat my Long COVID. During the first two days at the clinic, multiple brain scans and images were taken. On day three, I met with a psychiatrist, Dr. Robert Johnson, who explained my scans and came up with a treatment plan for my mental health.

Dr. Johnson was wonderful. One particularly challenging day, I was speaking to him and explained that my life had felt like torture for too long because of COVID. I also expressed anxiety about what I would have to face in the future. Life seems to get harder as you get older, and I wasn't even 30 yet! Dr. Johnson had the most genuine, kind response. He inquired about my spiritual health and went on to say that this challenge was setting me up for a life that would be happy. He reminded me that something simple, like eating an apple, would bring me joy. He reminded me that I probably wouldn't take too many things for granted, because I now knew exactly how important each of the five senses is. He reminded me that I wouldn't have a hard time finding things to be grateful for and that my Long COVID experience would likely be one of the most difficult trials I would face in my life.

A few months later, in November 2023, I decided that it was time to try another round of SGBs. Since the first time I saw the Facebook post about them by David Gaskins, the CRNA in Texas, I had come to know some of his patients and followed their experiences. David had the most knowledge and clinical experience about how to make these blocks work for parosmiacs specifically. I had already traveled around the country for treatment, so I decided that it would be worth the trip just to speak with him and get his perspective. It wasn't long before we were on a plane to Austin and making the drive to Bryan just to see him. Walking into the office felt like a breath of fresh air. No one discounted my experience. Everyone who worked there had seen patients come and go who were experiencing the same thing that I was.

There's a scripture posted on the wall directly behind the front desk of David's office. The verse comes from Joshua 24:15. It states, "As for me and my house, we will serve the Lord." Before performing the first block, David explained that he knew that this treatment had helped so many people who were struggling, just like I was. He also told me that he knew he was here to facilitate help, but that the Lord deserved the glory of any success that he had. David is an amazing medical professional and person. He truly cares about his patients and finding ways to help them. He gave away hundreds of thousands of dollars' worth of these blocks just to gain more clinical experience and figure out the best way to perform them that would offer the most relief for as many patients as possible. After consulting with him, I knew that David was the right person to administer this round of SGBs. I needed to hear about his confidence in the Lord. After speaking with him, I was reminded that we are on the Lord's timeline. We have a responsibility to do what we can, and even if it isn't working, we have to keep trying and not give up. There's a reason we go through challenges, even if it is only to help those who come after us. I still wasn't tasting or smelling normally after this round of blocks, but I remember saying that I would be okay if my taste or smell never improved from where it was at that moment.

When we got home from Texas, I had a few good weeks. Then Jayden and I contracted both Influenza A and B and were very sick. This reset everything, and we were back to the starting line, again. At this point, I had been living with parosmia for over two years and felt like it would never end. It took me a while to want to try another round of nerve blocks, but in October 2024, we went back to Texas. It was nice to see David and his staff again and rekindle my hope. As we chatted, he remembered that we were from Utah. He told me that there was an office in Boise, ID, where he had some colleagues whom he trusted completely, and I could go there if I ever wanted or needed to do more SGBs. Boise is still a ways away from where we lived, about six hours in a car, but it was closer than Bryan. He was so willing to help me find care, even if it wasn't from him.

At this point, I was eager to continue trying. I wondered if having more injections closer together would be helpful. During the next two months, Jayden and I travelled to Boise to test my theory. At this office, we met Annie Carr and Josh Coleman. Both of these providers are incredible, just like David said. They want all of their patients to have success stories and will do anything in their power to help. I received blocks from both Annie and Josh, and they were the easiest, least painful blocks I had ever experienced... And they helped! No smells or tastes were normal or even good yet, but I was finally feeling like I had made some progress.

During this time, I also decided to resign from my job as Career Advisor to focus on regaining my health. There are not enough wonderful things that I can say about my friend and former supervisor, Lisa Laird. She was an incredible support to me during my time at Snow College. She understood why I needed to travel to these different clinics, and most importantly, she encouraged me to continue doing so. Lisa would remind me that taking time off wasn't a big deal, and it was the reason why we were given both sick and vacation time. I have never had a boss like her. Even when I tried to quit my job in the fall of 2024, she encouraged me to complete all of the documentation that HR would need to put me on medical leave. Doing this would allow me to keep all of my appointments, take advantage of my PTO, and still have a job to return to if I wanted to come back. She also let me know that it was fine if I still wanted to submit my letter of resignation after I returned to work. Ultimately, I did end up resigning from that job in January of 2025. I will forever be grateful for her example and kindness throughout my time at the Snow College Career Center.

In February 2025, part of my family was going on a trip to San Antonio, TX. Jayden and I decided to take the "long way" to San Antonio and go through Bryan again. David administered another round of SGBs. During our time in San Antonio, I was able to eat a turkey sandwich for the first time in three years! This was the moment I realized Dr. Johnson had been spot on when he told me that this challenge was setting me up for a life where I would find joy in the smallest things. I have no idea how many times we have been in a restaurant where the food has made me cry. It's so much better when I begin to cry because I can eat instead of having the smells feel like a punch in the nose that instantly brings me to tears.

I can never thank my family, friends, and medical providers enough for the support, hope, and encouragement that they have given me. There are no words to express how grateful I am for my husband, my parents, my brothers and their wives, and my sweet nephews and nieces. They have all played a role in my not giving up on this Long COVID journey. They have wholeheartedly supported me through my struggle by sharing new information, cooking different meals, helping with finances, continually encouraging me, and understanding why I didn't want to be at Thanksgiving or Christmas. They never question me when I say that I want to try a new treatment or have a wild idea that "might help." I know that no matter what the outcome is, they will be cheering for me while I try, and pick me up if it doesn't work out like I had hoped. I am convinced that there isn't anyone on this planet who is luckier than I am when it comes to having such a wonderful family.

Throughout my experience, I have learned that everyone has something to offer, whether it's support, advice, or stories of personal experiences. Each person you meet knows something that you don't. Everyone has a story to share and something to teach if you are vulnerable enough to ask. Your circle can expand very quickly, and it can lift and support you when needed. Succeeding on your own can be challenging, but having a solid support system can keep you going and continually give you hope as you live your life. It is essential to find people whom you can rely on as you are on your journey. Make time and show that you care about them and want them to succeed, too. You never know when a person's trajectory will change because of a quick text or phone call to check in. If you show your support for others, they will likely support you, too. Be patient, be open, and be willing to talk and listen. Your network will continue to grow, and you will be able to find more life-changing friends and opportunities.

As I write this in the summer of 2025, three and a half years in, I am still not close to normal. I have had over 30 Stellate Ganglion Blocks, nine iron infusions, multiple ozone dialysis sessions, hyperbaric oxygen treatments, and PRP treatments, many brain scans, nasal scopes, and ultrasounds, months of intense supplementation, and countless doctor visits. I am making slow progress. I believe that one day, I will be normal again. Whether or not success comes quickly, your support system will always be there to provide hope and encouragement.

"Helping one person might not change the whole world, but it could change the world for one person."

– Unknown

While most kids were playing with action figures, Eric LeVine was in the kitchen testing and tasting recipes. As a youngster growing up in Brooklyn, Eric found excitement, challenges, and passion in his favorite place—the kitchen.

His childhood love became his career path and purpose, which led him  to The Culinary Institute of America in Hyde Park, New York. Soon after graduation, LeVine, worked under celebrated chef David Burke at the River Café, an experience he credits with sparking his creative artistry with food. Throughout his career, LeVine has focused on melding old-world techniques with modern innovation, skills he learned from top chefs worldwide but mastered as his very own along the way

LeVine has been recognized by the James Beard Foundation with two nominations—Southeast Chef of the Year and Outstanding Chef—and has earned numerous other top honors. These include Creative Caterer of the Year and Chef of the Year from the International Chef's Association, as well as Best Chef Long Island (2023 and 2024) and Best American Restaurant Long Island 2024 for his restaurant, 317 Main.

Chef LeVine is Chef/Partner of six restaurants, including 317 Main Street, Vico, The James Room, The Nutty Irishman + Stage 317. He has been featured in numerous publications, including Wine Spectator, USA Today, The New York Times, with a coveted 3-star review, and various industry magazines. LeVine's network appearances include NBC, ABC, CBS, Beat Bobby Flay, Alex vs. America, and a Chopped Championship honor on Food Network. He has authored four cookbooks, including *Stick It, Spoon It, Put It in a Glass, SMALL BITES BIG FLAVORS, Burgers, Bowls,* and *Jars and Forkin' Good.*

Beyond the kitchen, Eric is a six-time cancer survivor and passionate advocate for cancer research, a deeply personal cause he embraced after the loss of his brother. In November 2024, he fulfilled a lifelong dream—running his first marathon in his brother's honor, proving that his fight extends far beyond food.

CHAPTER 11
Sharing. Listening. Learning.

Introduction:

My name is Chef Eric LeVine, and I have spent my career pushing the boundaries of culinary creativity while building meaningful connections in the food industry. Over the years, I've had the privilege of leading acclaimed kitchens, authoring cookbooks, and winning prestigious culinary awards. My journey has taken me from high-pressure competition stages to intimate dining experiences, always fueled by a passion for innovation, flavor, and storytelling through food.

Networking has been a vital part of my professional and personal growth. In the culinary world, relationships open doors to collaborations, mentorship, and opportunities to share ideas that inspire and elevate the craft. Whether it's partnering with local farmers, engaging with fellow chefs, or connecting with guests, each relationship strengthens my ability to create memorable dining experiences. For me, networking isn't just about business—it's about building a community where we learn from one another and grow together.

Chapter Thesis:

In the culinary world, your skills can get you in the door, but it's the relationships you build that determine how far you'll go. Over the years, I've learned that the conversations in the dining room, the quiet advice from a mentor, and the unexpected collaboration with a peer can shape your career as much as the recipes you master. Networking isn't about chasing opportunities—it's about creating them through genuine connection. True networking in the culinary world is not about collecting contacts, but about cultivating authentic relationships built on trust, generosity, and mutual growth. My journey has shown that the most valuable opportunities come not from who you know, but from those who know, respect, and believe in you.

Section 1: The Context

Coming into the restaurant business at a young age (11 years old), it wasn't easy to get someone to listen to me, mentor me, or guide me. I was on my own.

I had to learn to be resourceful and find the answers that no one wanted to share.

When and Where:

In the early 2000s, after battling through personal and professional setbacks, I found myself at a crossroads in my career. I had the skills, the passion, and a track record of success, but I needed new opportunities to rebuild my presence in the culinary world. This phase truly crystallized during my involvement in national culinary competitions and industry charity events in New York and across the country.

Initial Challenges:

I faced two major challenges. First, I was emerging from a period where my name wasn't as visible in the public eye—new chefs and trends were capturing the spotlight. Second, I needed to reestablish my credibility and relevance in a rapidly evolving industry. Networking was not just about finding the next job; it was about reconnecting with old peers, forging new relationships, and showing the industry I was still here, still hungry, and still capable of delivering something unique. By putting myself in rooms filled with decision-makers, media, and fellow chefs, I began to rebuild my reputation one conversation, one handshake, and one shared dish at a time.

Section 2: Your Story / The Networking Journey

When I first started out, I didn't have a PR team or a big marketing budget—what I had was my food, my story, and a genuine passion for connecting with people. Social media became my stage. I'd post photos fresh from the kitchen, behind-the-scenes moments, and the stories behind my dishes. It wasn't about "selling" my restaurants—it was about inviting people into my world.

I also made it a point to show up in person—whether it was a local food event, a charity fundraiser, or a collaborative dinner with another chef. Each conversation was an opportunity, not just to talk about my cooking, but to listen, learn, and find common ground.

The biggest lesson I learned early on? Networking isn't a transaction—it's a relationship. When you approach it with authenticity, people remember not just what you do, but who you are. And that's what keeps them coming back—both to your table and to your story.

Early on, I realized that networking isn't just about promoting yourself—it's about building genuine relationships. I learned the importance of engaging with people authentically, listening to their stories, and finding ways to offer value before asking for anything in return. This mindset turned social media from just a broadcasting tool into a conversation space where real connections could grow.

Using social media has been my most powerful tool for sharing my craft and telling the story behind my food. It allows me to showcase my restaurants in a way that feels authentic—giving people a taste of the passion, creativity, and dedication that goes into every dish.

One of the most pivotal connections in my career came when I met a fellow chef at a charity food event. I was plating dishes in a fast-paced, high-energy kitchen when he walked over to compliment my work. We struck up a conversation—not about business, but about our shared love for bold flavors and pushing culinary boundaries.

That single conversation turned into a friendship, and eventually, a professional collaboration that opened doors I never could have imagined. We cooked side by side at events, shared ideas, and supported each other's ventures. Looking back, it wasn't just about meeting someone influential—it was about finding someone whose passion matched my own. That's when I realized that the best connections are built on shared values, not just opportunity.

1. **The Food Critic at the Farmers Market**

   I was walking through a local farmers' market, talking with growers about their produce, when I noticed someone quietly observing my conversations. She introduced herself as a food critic who had heard about my restaurant but had never visited. Instead of giving her a formal pitch, I invited her to the kitchen that afternoon to taste what I was cooking with those same market ingredients. She came, she ate, and a week later, her glowing review brought in a wave of new guests. That day reminded me that authenticity sells better than any advertisement.

2. **The Restaurateur at a Culinary Competition**

   During a national culinary competition, I was laser-focused on the dishes—until one of the judges struck up a conversation with me during a break. He wasn't just a judge—he was a veteran restaurateur with decades of experience. After the competition, we kept in touch, and his mentorship became a guiding force for me. He didn't just teach me about running a restaurant—he taught me about resilience, balance, and staying true to my culinary vision.

3. The Instagram Connection Turned Collaboration

One night, I received a direct message from a pastry chef I'd never met. She had been following my work on Instagram and loved the way I approached flavor combinations. We decided to meet for coffee, which turned into a brainstorming session that became a sold-out dessert and wine pairing event at my restaurant. That partnership not only boosted our profiles but showed me how powerful digital connections can be when you take them into the real world.

Over time, these relationships became more than professional connections—they became a support system. The critic who first tasted my food at the farmers market continued to champion my work, helping to build my restaurant's reputation. The restaurateur I met at the competition became a trusted mentor, guiding me through both growth and challenges in the industry. The pastry chef I collaborated with pushed me creatively, inspiring me to explore flavors and presentations I might never have considered on my own.

Each of these connections brought new opportunities, but more importantly, they reminded me that my journey is not a solo act. Every dish I create, every event I host, carries the fingerprints of the people who've influenced, supported, and believed in me along the way. Those relationships didn't just affect my career—they shaped who I am as a chef and as a person.

One of the most effective strategies I've used is storytelling—both in person and online. I don't just post a picture of a dish; I tell the story behind it—where the ingredients came from, what inspired the flavors, and the emotions I hope it will evoke. That authenticity creates a deeper connection with my audience.

Another key tactic has been consistency. Whether it's showing up at local charity events, collaborating with other chefs, or engaging daily on social media, I've learned that visibility and reliability build trust over time.

Over the years, I've adapted my networking style by paying attention to what resonates with people. If a post gets a lot of engagement, I'll explore that theme more. If an in-person event sparks meaningful conversations, I'll seek out similar opportunities. I've also learned to be more selective—focusing on quality interactions rather than trying to be everywhere at once. This shift has allowed me to build stronger, more authentic relationships that translate into real opportunities.

Section 3: The Results

Growth and Opportunities

Networking has directly fueled the growth of my business and opened doors I never imagined. From high-profile event invitations to collaborative dinners with chefs I admire, each connection has created new opportunities to showcase my work and expand my reach. Partnerships born from casual conversations have led to innovative menu creations, cross-promotions, and even joint ventures that brought fresh energy to my restaurants.

Personal Growth

Networking has changed me far beyond the business side. It's taught me the value of listening before speaking, of approaching every interaction with genuine curiosity rather than an agenda.

My communication skills have sharpened, my empathy has deepened, and I've become more strategic in how I follow up and nurture relationships.

On a personal level, these connections have enriched my life with friendships, mentorships, and experiences that extend well beyond the kitchen. I've shared meals, traveled, and celebrated milestones with people I would have never met without putting myself out there. Networking hasn't just shaped my career—it's made me a better leader, collaborator, and human being.

Life Changes

Networking hasn't just shaped my career—it's reshaped my life. Many of the people I've met through my culinary journey have become more than professional contacts; they've become lifelong friends and even extended family. I've celebrated weddings, attended milestone birthdays, and shared deeply personal moments with people I never would have known if I hadn't taken the time to connect.

It's also changed my perspective on success. I've come to see that the real reward of networking isn't just the opportunities— it's the relationships that enrich your life in ways you can't put a price on. The community I've built has been there to celebrate my wins and to lift me during challenges. That support network is something I'll carry with me for the rest of my life.

Section 4: Challenges and Lessons

Networking hasn't always been easy for me. In the beginning, time management was a huge hurdle. Running a kitchen and managing restaurants leaves little room for extra events or follow-ups, and I often felt stretched too thin to truly nurture new relationships.

I also had to push myself out of my comfort zone when it came to approaching people. As a chef, I was used to letting my food speak for me—but networking demanded that I speak for myself. That meant initiating conversations, sharing my story, and being vulnerable enough to face rejection. And yes, rejection happened. Not every interaction led to an opportunity, and some doors closed before they even opened.

What I learned, though, is that every "no" is just part of the process. By embracing the uncomfortable moments and learning from them, I became better at communicating, more strategic in choosing where to invest my time, and more confident in showing up as myself.

The way I navigated networking challenges was by reframing my mindset. Instead of seeing networking as a task on my to-do list, I started viewing it as an extension of what I love—sharing food, stories, and experiences with people. That shift made it feel natural rather than forced. I also became intentional about scheduling time for follow-ups, even if it was just sending a quick message or sharing an article someone might enjoy. Over time, those little efforts built trust and kept relationships alive.

Key Takeaways
Networking is less about collecting contacts and more about cultivating genuine connections. Be authentic, be consistent, and focus on listening as much as speaking.

Dos:

- Share your story in a way that connects emotionally.
- Follow up promptly and meaningfully.
- Look for ways to give before you ask for something in return.
- Show up—both online and in person—where your community is.

Don'ts:

- Don't approach networking as a one-time transaction.
- Don't dominate the conversation—make it a dialogue.
- Don't try to be everywhere at once; choose quality over quantity.
- Don't let rejection stop you—every "no" is just a step toward the next "yes."

Conclusion

Reflection

Networking has transformed my career and my life in ways I never expected. It's brought me opportunities that expanded my restaurants, introduced me to people who became lifelong friends, and inspired me to grow both as a chef and as a leader. The relationships I've built have been the driving force behind some of my proudest achievements—and the steady hand during my toughest moments.

Future Outlook

I see networking not as a phase in my career, but as an ongoing practice. My approach continues to evolve with the times—leveraging social media in new ways, attending targeted events that align with my vision, and seeking out collaborations that challenge my creativity. I'm more intentional than ever about surrounding myself with people who share my values and push me to be better.

Encouragement

If there's one thing I've learned, it's this: networking works best when it comes from a place of authenticity and generosity. Start small—reach out to someone you admire, attend one event, or share your passion online. Listen more than you speak, and focus on building relationships, not just contacts. You never know which conversation might change your career—or your life.

"Service to others is
the rent you pay for
your room here on
earth."

– Muhammad Ali

Sharon Birdsong Riddle brings more than 30 years of experience delivering strategic business solutions across corporate, nonprofit, and government sectors. She began her real estate journey in 2005, investing in single-family properties with her business partner and spouse, Dan. In 2015, the duo shifted their focus to multifamily investments and have since invested in 18 properties across multiple states.

Sharon is actively involved as a limited partner and is now pursuing general partner roles and additionally is well known in the real estate investment community for her leadership and networking. She is a committed member of several professional groups, including Women's Multifamily Mastermind, Wealth Wise Women, Brad Sumrok's personal mentoring program, Millionaire Multifamily Mastermind, and Hunter Thompson's Raisemasters mastermind.

Among her peers, she is affectionately known as the "Podcast Queen" for her frequent guest appearances on podcasts, engaging presence, and contributions. Her eBook "Spilling the Tea: Multifamily Investing Made Simple" will be launched in early Fall 2025. She has a goal of launching her own podcast in 2026 to be named "Spilling the Tea on Real Estate, Business, and Legacy".

Sharon holds a Bachelor of Applied Arts and Sciences in Rehabilitation Studies from the University of North Texas and an M.B.A. from the Satish & Yasmin Gupta College of Business, formerly the Graduate School of Management at the University of Dallas, with a focus on Business Administration and Management with additional elective hours in accounting and finance.

"Start each day with a cup of tea, a review of your accounts, a quick scan of networks for new opportunities, and review that smart investment plan you launched."
—Sharon Birdsong Riddle

CHAPTER 12

The Zombies or Dream Champions: Are you attracting the people you seek into your chosen rooms as part of your network? Is it your reality or a dream?

Introduction:

As a 3rd generation Texan, connection is vital. I am connected to the Birdsong, Becker, and Riddle families as I continue to live in my hometown of Denton, Texas, a two-college city. My name is Sharon Riddle.

As a Dentonite, I live with my spouse, Dan, in a ranch-style home. We are on almost an acre. At our home, there are several mature oaks, rabbits, hawks, wood lizards, and occasionally snakes. Coyotes do roam and, at times, howl.

Dan and I have a 28-year-old daughter who will join us as a partner in a real estate LLC in 2025–2026. She, too, is a Dentonite. Additionally, Dan and I are actively involved in church, local, regional, and global charities.

Over my professional career, which began in 1981, I worked in companies, nonprofit organizations, and government agencies. As a commuting professional, I provided business solutions in the areas of software upgrades and business process analyses, and conducted best business practice research. I had business colleagues from various backgrounds, cultures, and educations with differing personalities. Sometimes I used my background as a 3rd generation Texan to keep me both grounded and unique while adding in some of my Texas Grit. I still do.

Then in 2005, I began investing in single-family real estate with my spouse and business partner, Dan. I took a leadership role in managing all facets of this business. I became an entrepreneur, often managing teams of contractors for my fledgling company. During this time, I relied on formal real estate education, my MBA coursework, and lessons I learned from my entrepreneurial family. This included my mom and dad, uncles, and aunts. I even had a childhood neighbor who was a business owner of the only toy store in Denton, Texas, and a real estate investor herself!

Dan and I started the transition to multifamily real estate in 2015 through initial education and investing passively in 18 properties in Texas, Oklahoma, Colorado, Florida, and Ohio, totaling 3,507 units to date. We needed more doors and a business that could better scale in terms of profits, too.

I received my early networking education from both my Grandmother Becker and Grandmother Birdsong. These wise women understood the value and power of networking and shared this with me as a child. Both women were collaborators for the common good, pillars of their communities, and never forgot a face or name. I mastered their life lessons.

Coming from a then small Texas college town with one high school where football was played well, I grew up very connected to people, places, and later the Denton High School Bronco Band. My early dream champions came from within the youth and adults of this band. Only a few zombies came from this tribe and time!

During and after college, I met or knew people who could or would offer me a job. Since I pounded the pavement very hard in the early 1980s, my later dream champions helped successfully launch me in a career as a young professional woman.

Networking has become and remains a vital part of my life. My network is even more critical for my business successes, drives my companies' expansions, and increases profits. I use my network as a resource in order to better vet business partners. So, as you can see, your network truly is your net worth.

As I continue to increase the number of my dream champions through my two real estate masterminds, Millionaire Multifamily Mastermind and RaiseMasters, the connections multiply exponentially. Many are long-lasting. I met one of my mentors, Brad Sumrok, almost 10 years ago. Hunter Thompson was referred to me over a year ago. I grow my vendor team, partners, and my investors through my network or by networking.

Remember, you have the power to attract the people you seek in virtual or in-person rooms.

Section 1: The Early Rooms

I truly embraced networking upon graduation from college. It was the 1980s, and I pounded the pavement very hard. This was probably the most challenging time of my early career. I felt I was struggling to even launch! I was not, however, entirely friendless. My family connections landed me my first two jobs.

I quickly realized that my limited family connections could only help me in the beginning of my career. With my first job at ARCO Oil and Gas in Dallas, Texas, I networked at CAP Luncheons. These luncheons were attended by mostly males.

I took those opportunities to get to know my co-workers better, interact with employees from other departments, and learn about volunteer opportunities as well. A smile and a firm handshake were required.

I also began to understand that this was my very first time using a pivot. Once you leverage who you know with what you know, you could repeat this process. It opened the doors to the rooms I chose and my chosen employers as well. After I received my MBA, my knowledge could be leveraged more. The human connection never went away. If I were likable, then I would be hired. It was the subjective part of the hiring process.

At this time in my career, all the networking rooms were in-person. It was a cumbersome process! You had to call in to register for a networking event and then drive to the event, park the car, sit in an uncomfortable chair, and then rapidly meet strangers. It was a bit like speed dating! Sometimes it was just as effective.

Still, those events gave me some visibility and opportunities to rehearse my pitch. I was the brand. Sometimes I had to grit my way through some impostor syndrome.

Reflecting upon the networking opportunities at this time in my career, I found them lacking in tools, tips, tricks, and hacks. Those would need to come at a much later time.

Section 2: Shy Construction Brat to Energetic Committed Networker and Podcast Guest

My early methods of networking were all in-person and rather clumsy. These were mostly trial and error. Perhaps sales employees had more formal networking training. I was never in that profession. I confess I was undereducated in successful networking strategies. I did not continue to underutilize that skill.

An additional strategic outcome of the in-person method of networking is meeting one of my mentors, Brad Sumrok. I met him at his Rat Race to Retirement event. I have worked with him for almost a decade on multifamily real estate coaching and mentoring. His mastermind is Millionaire Multifamily Mastermind. I significantly increased my net worth through this network.

Meeting a mentor is certainly a key encounter. Having two mentors is even better! Each has a unique skill set to teach.

I met my second mentor at his in-person event as well. I was referred by one of his mentees. That mentor is Hunter Thompson. His event is RaiseFest, and his mastermind is RaiseMasters.

I also knew Greg Butcher, a RaiseMaster, from Brad Sumrok's community. Greg referred me to RaiseMasters. He knew I wanted to improve my capital raising skills. Knowing Greg opened doors to me with RaiseMasters.

I still attend in-person events. All my mastermind events are in-person. Those events always improve my business opportunities and increase both my network and net worth. After a conversation with my former stage broker, I realized there is also a hunger for live events.

I mentally rehearse for virtual and in-person events. This is a skill I have amplified further in the last two years. You can learn so much about visualization even on YouTube!

Additionally, I seek to introduce myself to others while intentionally being the best version of myself. This includes dress, face, voice, active listening skills, mindset, energy, and mood.

Now I have expanded my networking strategy to joining online communities. It's a one-to-many networking strategy with improved outcomes. I needed a new strategy. John Laine, also a RaiseMaster, encouraged me to try this strategy.

These days, I network on Facebook, Instagram, and LinkedIn. I post and set appointments from contacts on these three social media platforms for business appointments and podcasts. My learning curve was steep in 2024 on LinkedIn. I had to go to coaching calls and review RaiseMaster modules to gain some mastery. Consistency is key to mastery!

Also, I join groups or communities on Facebook and LinkedIn. Even a podcaster and podcast guest community!

Furthermore, I use Slack, Zoom, and WhatsApp for my masterminds and summits. I guess we can all thank the COVID-19 pandemic for the numerous virtual events. I am thankful for Zoom!

John Laine and I are continuing to discuss conversion rates. How can I create investors from appointments? This is an area of growth for me in 2025 and 2026.

One networking strategy I want to use in 2025–2026 is community service. I want to use this strategy to distribute wheelchairs for Chair the Love in the United States and overseas. This is a global charity I was first introduced to by Brad Sumrok in 2023. I was at his Millionaire Multifamily Mastermind in Punta de Mita, Mexico. It was a beautiful place, a lovely property, with people who shared my passion and a mentor helping me grow in yet another quadrant of my life.

Hunter Thompson introduced me to Baby2Baby at RaiseFest in February 2025 while I attended his event in Phoenix, Arizona. Now I'm a donor as part of my RaiseMaster community.

I'm sure there are other unexplored and worthy charities I want to place on my radar screen in the future. I want to bring a tribe to those events with me, just like my mentors do.

Strategic networking is non-negotiable. We build relationships with key industry players, gaining insights and opening doors to exclusive deals. The fact that I am contributing a chapter to this book is an outcome of strategic networking.

Section 3: The Results

Two of my business partners came from my network in Brad Sumrok's community. We tour target properties together and submit Letters of Intent for multifamily property acquisitions.

My marketing team came from a network. I watched Tim Crouch build a company, The Crouch Group, in Denton, Texas. I previously worked with Tim at Cox Cable. I was a co-op intern while working on my MBA, and he was the production manager.

I also have coaches and business friends who help me increase my AI skills. Their tools, tips, tricks, and hacks shave time off my learning curve. It has become an AI user network.

When I attend mastermind events, I expect to have business opportunities presented to me. This frequently occurs.

Setting expectations is critical. I am now exploring a business opportunity with a podcaster. She is using a real estate business model in the split pad space.

My podcaster network has dramatically improved my follow-up skills. It's not just about the guest interview. Follow-up is needed for content production. The podcast content is sent to my marketing team and uploaded to YouTube. After having been on many podcast guest interviews, I believe Ken Walls is a master of the podcast process.

I am now a member of a Facebook group for podcasters and podcast guests. How did this happen? I was referred to this Facebook group by a podcaster.

Being a podcast guest has truly honed my communication skills and strategic thinking. I outline critical topics I want to discuss and how I want the audience to contact me. Additionally, I pitch my future eBook and this book as well!

I have also increased my empathy when there are some technical difficulties on a podcast. I've been in a podcaster's shoes. I have had technical difficulties, resolved those, and rescheduled to deliver a successful podcast guest interview. The key is to be flexible and to have some grace!

That is not all. During a Millionaire Multifamily Mastermind, we spent time at a health and fitness resort, Movara. At that resort, I found my nutritionist and fitness coach, Andre Shook, RD, CD, CPT, LWM. This continues to be life-changing. I hired Andre. He will help me position myself to be the fittest and strongest version of myself. I will "get to Greece" in 2028 for a mother/daughter trip. Remember, health is the companion of wealth!

Section 4: Challenges and Lessons

Thanks to my grandmothers, I learned to speak with people at an early age. I choose to be sympathetic to those who face more challenges in public speaking or networking. I have family members who face those challenges daily.

Some of my early obstacles began at the start of my professional career. Minimal professional networking experiences and strategies led to frustration and rejection. I only had in-person events at my disposal.

It was a cumbersome process! I had to call in to register for a networking event and then drive to the event, park the car, sit in an uncomfortable chair, and then rapidly meet strangers. It was a bit like speed dating! Sometimes it was just as effective.

I now use humor more than ever as an ice breaker. As a frequent podcast guest, I always seem to have a story to share. A laugh certainly relieves stress and the feeling of overwhelm.

Additionally, as a key takeaway, I praise publicly and correct privately in all my networks, especially my two masterminds. This solution is currently to affirm and not alienate those individuals who just do not totally align with my actions or core values.

Sometimes you will be rejected. Some people will not connect with you on social media or initiate personal contact with you in a crowded or not-so-crowded room. It stings. Go ahead and detach. Keep in mind, I am a modern-age Stoic.

This rejection can occur with podcasters, too. I've been ghosted or sent a direct message (DM) that the producer does not believe I am a good fit for a podcast. I had to remove the podcaster from my network and unsubscribe from a newsletter the podcaster published. At times, less contact is best. Tact is so vital for business networking!

My current challenge in networking is how to maintain a professional relationship with people who do not always align with my values. This becomes even more challenging within my two mastermind communities. Masterminds are selective by design of the mentor. Selective does not need to be elitist. The mentor should ensure the mastermind environment is inviting and that newer members can navigate with ease.

Sometimes an individual, group, mastermind, or any network is no longer a good fit. It may be hard to say "Goodbye." If a mentor or a significant portion of a mastermind's members are no longer the best fit for you, go ahead and pause your membership. Keep in mind we all have more limiting beliefs and fears to conquer. Carl Jung, the father of modern-day psychoanalysis, called it "shadow work."

The same process applies to in-person or virtual networks. Remember that you are responsible for your own growth.

Conclusion:

Networking continues to positively impact my business and personal life. Sometimes it connects me with high-integrity and high-net-worth people outside my own network, like Bill Walsh. This requires focus and discipline.

I am grateful that networking has made huge strides since the early 1980s when I launched my professional career. Zoom continues to be a godsend for me in business. I am certain it is for many others.

Furthermore, I highly recommend adding a coach or mentor to your own network. Both coaches and mentors have networks or masterminds or both. This enlarges your own network and creates time savings.

My business partner and I are also sponsors of a real estate networking group. It is a REIA. That group is 1REClub in Fort Worth, Texas. One of our early real estate coaches, Jimmy Reed, is the organizer. Jimmy continues to give us opportunities. We are glad to pay it forward.

Currently, Brad Sumrok and Hunter Thompson are my real estate mentors. Each one has a unique skill set and emphasis, along with a network and a mastermind. These align with my actions and goals. My current goals are the expansion of my real estate investments and to assist 100 individuals or families to become multifamily real estate investors in 24 months.

What will my future networks look like? I do not have all the answers. What I do understand about myself is that I want creative solutions to problems. Where are the people with networks that provide solutions? I want to connect with them.

I also believe more charities will be part of my future networks. I need to fully explore this networking technique to determine how it fits in my overall business strategy. It seems to hold untapped potential for my business partner and me currently.

Go ahead and upgrade or add to your cross-skills with a coach or mentor. I have a mentor who is totally committed to time blocking and Artificial Intelligence (AI). Time blocking can free up blocks of time for networking. AI has limitless potential for use in our lives and businesses.

Always choose or create your network wisely. Be a business promoter of your business or charity! Find a champion. Keep learning new skills and ideas. Networking is evolving. Stay informed of new tips, techniques, tools, and hacks. Many clubs or industries offer networking chapters with speakers and networking opportunities.

Be aware that many podcasters are also coaches. Being a guest on a podcast can open opportunities most people do not even know exist. Thank you to Ken Walls for affording me this opportunity to be an author of this book.

I look forward to sharing more of my journey and even more takeaways on Facebook, Instagram, and LinkedIn. I post daily. Also, contact me via my company website at www.excalibretexas.com where I blog.

I was raised in a home that was kind of like the TV show 'Green Acres'. My mom loved comfort, and my dad loved the outdoors. So, naturally, I love both too. Although I wouldn't say I grew up each day with a

silver spoon or having to use an outhouse at o dark-thirty in freezing cold conditions complete with the Sears catalog, my experiences have run the complete range. And, I've loved every minute of it. From camping across the USA three separate times to spending a long weekend as a guest at a billionaire's compound. I've seen and experienced much in this life so far.

Here's what I know: Enjoying one's life is the goal. Making the best of each day and deciding to be happy is really the pinnacle of success. For me, relationships with people are the most rewarding and joyful. I love animals too. Work is important but not the primary mission. I love stories. So, when we meet, let's take some time to share one or two. Talk soon. Jim

Presently, I'm promoting Lisa Loree - The Rebel Ballerina and her work helping single moms to break free and create a beautiful family legacy for themselves. Download Lisa's latest ebook here:

https://www.rebelfawn.com/ebook01

CHAPTER 13
Network Effects To Deliver Real Longevity

Introduction: A Fork in the Road

It was, for me, the fateful day of February 10, 2020, that started like any other. Looking back, I now see it as a true fork in the road of my life. And boy, am I glad I know some amazing people and am indeed blessed to consider them friends.

What I decided to do was attempt, at all costs, to regain an intimate and very personal relationship—even though I was told in no uncertain terms that it was over.

You see, my body filed "divorce papers" on me, and our trial separation began that day.

You might be asking yourself, "What... is this guy nuts?"

Since then, I've been working to understand why, to fix, and then heal the injuries that completely altered my life's path and continue doing so today. I sincerely thought my amazing and active life experience, as I knew it, was over. On this day, my body indeed filed those divorce papers. It was also the day network effects became very real and very necessary.

This isn't just a story about success in business, although I've experienced a fair measure. It's about dropping everything and doing what it takes to make the necessary changes my body was demanding. I found it to be a rather engaging negotiation.

Section 1: Awakening Through Crisis

"Life's most persistent and urgent question is, 'What are you doing for others?'" – Martin Luther King Jr.

Chances are high that while living in the United States today, you and I are in serious health trouble. According to recent studies, approximately 88% of the U.S. population—over 300 million people—is on a debilitating and potentially deadly path to chronic disease. The common name for this condition is "metabolic syndrome," a progressive disorder that begins subtly but escalates to pre-diabetes, diabetes, Alzheimer's, cardiovascular disease, and much more.

I know firsthand because I've been there. Yet, today, many of us thrive despite this challenge. We're reversing it through collective knowledge, empowering each other, and embracing wisdom from pioneering medical heroes like Dr. William Davis, Dr. Jason Fung, and Dr. Steven Gundry. Network effects have proven not only transformative but life-saving.

Section 2: Recognizing the Hidden Epidemic

"I believe in integrity. Dogs have it. Humans are sometimes lacking it." – Cesar Millan

Medical evidence now clearly links conditions such as Alzheimer's, multiple sclerosis, heart disease, cancer, dementia, and depression to metabolic syndrome. Yet, conventional healthcare remains alarmingly focused on profit rather than holistic solutions. Big pharma and entrenched medical practices often obscure simpler, self-managed treatments behind a curtain of complexity.

Understanding the scale of this epidemic was pivotal in my journey. Only after realizing that my health issues were part of a larger, systemic problem could I tap into networks capable of offering genuine solutions. Recognizing this hidden epidemic empowered me to pivot toward personal and community-driven healing.

Section 3: Building Your Personal Network

"Your network is your net worth." – Porter Gale

In life, just as in business, the relationships you cultivate become your greatest assets. When crisis struck, I instinctively turned to my network—built through decades of genuine connection, trust, and reciprocal support. My friends, colleagues, and professional contacts provided knowledge, emotional support, and resources that were crucial during those initial, daunting days.

Your personal network isn't just a list of contacts. It's a vibrant, supportive community capable of pulling you through crises. Whether facing health setbacks or professional hurdles, intentionally nurturing these relationships enriches your life beyond measure.

Section 4: The Power of Shared Knowledge

"Alone we can do so little; together we can do so much." – Helen Keller

When traditional healthcare fell short, my network came through. I immersed myself in Functional Medicine, learning from doctors and community members who openly shared their experiences and insights online. This collective wisdom—available through books, videos, forums, and personal exchanges—quickly illuminated pathways to healing that conventional methods overlooked.

The network effect here is potent: individual experiences become shared wisdom. Knowledge spreads rapidly, enabling more people to reclaim their health faster and more effectively than ever before.

Section 5: Taking 100% Responsibility

"Take care of your body. It's the only place you have to live." – Jim Rohn

Taking complete responsibility for my health was both terrifying and liberating. Instead of outsourcing my well-being entirely to doctors, I embraced accountability for my choices, habits, and diet. This responsibility triggered significant lifestyle shifts: intermittent fasting, improved dietary choices, and regular self-assessment.

By accepting full responsibility, I was no longer passive. Instead, I became empowered, actively engaging with the insights gleaned from my network. It's this mindset shift—total ownership—that accelerates personal healing and creates lasting change.

Section 6: Technological Amplification of Network Effects

"Technology is nothing. What's important is that you have faith in people." – Steve Jobs

Technology played a pivotal role in amplifying network effects during my journey. Platforms like YouTube, podcasts, and specialized online groups provided easy, rapid access to revolutionary medical insights and personal success stories. Without these resources, my path to recovery might have taken years longer—or might never have begun at all.

Through technology, wisdom previously confined to small, exclusive circles became universally accessible. This democratization of knowledge means anyone can leverage network effects for transformative personal growth and healing.

Section 7: Practical Steps for Creating Network Effect Momentum

"Momentum begets momentum, and the best way to start is to start." – Gil Penchina

Building powerful network effects requires intentional, consistent effort. Start by connecting deeply with others around shared goals or challenges. Offer genuine support, freely sharing your knowledge and resources without expectation. Over time, reciprocity naturally emerges, fueling momentum that collectively elevates everyone involved.

For me, simple acts like joining online health forums, initiating meaningful conversations, and generously sharing my own experiences created ripple effects that grew exponentially over time. Each step built upon the last, resulting in sustained, community-wide success.

Section 8: Expanding Beyond Yourself— Community Transformation

"The greatness of a community is most accurately measured by the compassionate actions of its members." – Coretta Scott King

The true power of network effects emerges when individual improvements cascade outward, transforming entire communities. I've witnessed remarkable communal transformations driven by shared health initiatives—groups collectively reducing obesity rates, reversing diabetes symptoms, and significantly lowering chronic disease risks.

By extending personal successes outward, we contribute to healthier, happier, and more resilient communities. This kind of transformation transcends personal gain, creating enduring legacies that benefit everyone.

Section 9: Leaving a Legacy of Chronic Health

"Legacy is not leaving something for people. It's leaving something in people." – Peter Strople

Now, at 67, having reclaimed my health and vitality, I'm committed to leaving a legacy of chronic health—sustainable wellness rather than chronic illness. This legacy involves actively teaching and sharing the knowledge I've accumulated. By encouraging others to adopt a learn-do-teach approach, network effects perpetuate indefinitely, spreading awareness and action widely and deeply.

Through collective engagement and continuous sharing, we ensure our communities not only survive but thrive, transforming how health is perceived and achieved for generations to come.

Conclusion: The Journey Ahead—Empowering, Joyful, and Collective

Harnessing network effects is more than a powerful strategy— it's an enriching, enjoyable, and profoundly meaningful way to live. My journey revealed the transformative potential of genuine, reciprocal relationships and collective wisdom. By embracing this interconnected way of living, challenges become opportunities, and crises transform into powerful catalysts for growth.

Today, network effects shape my daily life, making each step forward not only possible but profoundly enjoyable. Together, we create a vibrant web of support, empowering ourselves and each other on our shared journey through life. The path ahead is brighter, healthier, and infinitely more fulfilling when traveled together.

"Help others achieve
their dreams and you
will achieve yours."

– Les Brown

Lisa Loree is a professional ballerina, author, speaker, mentor, mom, friend, and lover, who lives in Southern California with her two adult kids and three grandkitties.

https://www.rebelfawn.com/ebook01

CHAPTER 14

Rebel Against the Lies: Creating the Life You Deserve

Life is amazing! Life is full of wonder and inspiration. But I didn't always feel this way. I did not view my life as an incredible gift. I didn't see my life as a gift at all. It was more of a chore. I would literally be irritated upon the opening of my eyes to a new day. Ugh. I'm still here.

Not only did I make my dream of being a professional ballerina come true, but I also lost that dream, as well as experiencing other tragedies, heartaches, and challenges. I've been at the very bottom. Depression and anxiety were my closest companions. Life had lost its luster, and I really didn't give a shit about what happened to me. I was stuck in a vicious cycle—you know—sun up, sun down. What on Earth was the purpose of even being on Earth? Who cares?

As a kid, I always knew I was going to be a ballerina. Yep. Since I was three years old, I knew. It wasn't a wish or a hope; it was a knowing. And I backed that understanding with years and years of hardcore training. Always at the studio instead of hanging out at the mall or whatever. I can't say I wasn't hanging out with my friends, because my fellow dance students were my friends, and we were with each other day in and day out. And then I had a remarkable opportunity to move to New York City to pursue the fulfillment of this knowing. Actually, I asked out of the blue to audition for a company that was touring through my hometown. And after being at their school for a year, I asked again.

The moral of the story in my story is to ask. You want something? Ask! So many opportunities are just waiting for the taking, but they won't happen until you make it happen. Ask and you shall receive. I had no idea how all that worked. I just knew I was going to be a ballerina, and that was that. But be very careful what you ask for!

There are lots of things I didn't know I was asking for that I did not want—but again, I didn't realize how all that was happening. So, I got that too, in many big and disastrous ways that brought extraordinary heartache and despair. Granted, I'm not giving details here to the depth of the tragedies I experienced, so you may not get a real sense of how low "low" really is. It's waaay lower than the limbo-party game of "How low can you go?" But you can read all about it in my very raw, uncut book, *Rebel Ballerina*, coming soon. There you will also find out in way more detail why I can now say enthusiastically, "Life is amazing!"

The first thing I did to bring change—or to bring things around—was rebel. Yep, I rebelled big time. But I figured, "Hey! Why not? I already have one foot in the grave, so what does it matter? What if I did what I wanted for once?" And then I Marine-crawled away from my now ex-husband. Not literally on my belly, but figuratively, that's exactly where I was. Eating dirt, with so very little of my soul left that I could not stand, not even be up on hands and knees. You might recognize this stance if you too have been so diminished that you have no words to utter.

The second thing I did was start hanging out with a rather new friend—and I didn't have many friends at this time. Ninety-five percent of the folks I thought were my friends proved they were not. Anyway, my friend and I went to a business networking event. Business wasn't really my thing, but I thought, "What the hell? I'm just biding my time anyway. I'll probably be bored, but it'll be a change of scenery." So we went, and during the course of this event, there was a speaker on the stage who said, "You create your life. Whether you have good things and like how it's going, or you have many, many challenges and are suffering, you created it." Not only was I stunned by these words, but I was also incensed. Thankfully, my sense of vanity and not wanting to be embarrassed kept me in my seat, but I really wanted to go up on that stage and punch him really hard! WTF? No one in their right mind would purposefully create the heaping shit life I was living! Who would do that?

That dramatic moment so grabbed my attention! This guy was doing an event of his own in a few months, and I was so intrigued that my friend and I went. From that, we joined his year-long mentorship program. Suddenly, I was surrounded by people who were not judging me and were living a very different life philosophy than what I had been raised with, and had followed my whole life. I felt a spark of life, like I was suddenly actually awake. And I wanted to be awake. Don't get me wrong, this was no snap-of-the-fingers and suddenly life was grand. But it put me on a path that said, "Go ahead, ask questions. Investigate. Be yourself! It's okay."

I began to understand how my thinking was wreaking havoc in my life. Things I didn't even realize I was thinking were playing in the background like a caustic, nearly silent, horrid rendering of static-y elevator music. Thoughts like, "You're not worthy. You're a failure. You're not good enough," ran through my mind subconsciously, and I had no idea how grating it was to my soul. You may still have your personal version of this playing in a low tone, in the very back of your awareness. Actually, unless you take action to correct this, I'm afraid you most certainly do.

It starts when we're really young through various messages—words, tone, body language—and from many different sources: parents, siblings, friends, belief systems, teachers, experiences, society at large, and more. And we have no idea how similar this is to the irritation one experiences while listening to fingernails scraping down a chalkboard. My apologies to those who went to school sometime after the 80s with the advent of the whiteboard, which is more squeaky than screechy. You may not relate to that detestable sound! Its discomfort is similar to a hangnail tear that we unknowingly add a grain of salt or drop of lemon juice to on such a regular basis that we've become numb to the pain. Or in cases like mine and other high-level athletes, where we don't even have normal pain responses anymore. I was informed by some researchers in a medical study that my pain neurology was different from the norm. I had actually turned off this function toward stupid little things, leaving only true injuries to register as needing attention. So it happens with the soul after hearing enough of this poisonous chatter. The problem is, even hangnails leave scarring, microscopic as it may be. Scars get in the way of normal, fluid functioning—be it muscles, skin, or emotions.

So what does our thinking have to do with networking? Only everything! What I didn't know at the time was that my initial rebellion put a stake in the ground—with some force, I might add. You can almost hear it vibrate out through the ethers, like the dramatic music of a movie, indicating massive change is about to happen. The downtrodden have found strength. A new struggle begins, but one that brings life and all kinds of victories along the way. It's vibrant! With that stake in the ground, I unwittingly declared that I matter.

With my new understanding ever-growing, I realized I needed to rebel against these negative thoughts that were eating through my soul like quick splashes of acid. These types of thoughts are 99 percent lies, by the way. What's playing on your old and worn-out record, tape, CD, streaming (can that get old and worn out?) are lies. And every time we think about them, they are emboldened with more neurology, creating deeper and tighter synapses that make them seem like reality. And because of this, they do become real, and you live these thoughts as reality. All thoughts are like that. The question is, which thoughts do you reinforce? Chances are great that unless you purposefully change these thoughts, they will dictate your life. And that is exactly how I ended up going through mountainous heartache, despair, and depression. Not on purpose, but by default, because I didn't understand how this works. And it's not like I could say, "But I didn't know, so take back all the misery!" No, I was fully living the consequences of what was set into motion by my thinking, unintentional or not. And unfortunately, other people were also living the fallout of my thoughts turned to choices.

But here's where it gets really, really good! I began to understand how my thoughts were leading me away from the life I really wanted, and that I could actually change that trajectory. I have the power to replace those old, corrosive thoughts that were bringing death with better, life-filled thoughts. Now again, I want to be clear. None of this happened overnight. I was and am relearning life, and that is indeed a process. It reminds me of the t-shirts you may have seen depicting evolution. They start with an image of a chimpanzee and show a progression of slouchy beings, transitioning from that chimpanzee into the human being that we recognize as such today. Personally, I don't believe in that particular transition. However, in my depiction, I start off as the puddle of muck crawling away from a life of guilt and buckets of tears, to crawling on hands and knees, to on my feet but slouchy, to upright, and even to dancing again. That is my progression, and I'm making my way back on stage where

I dance and speak my story. I hope to see you in the audience very soon!

You have this very same power. Everyone does. But this is no basic self-help razzmatazz. No, this takes actual work and consistency. It takes a willingness to become further unraveled in order to rebuild. It takes guts, grit, tenacity. You may have to grow some real gonads (ovaries are included in that term).

Let me break this down a little more for you. Those thoughts that have been rendering you helpless in your own life produced a life path of survival when you were very young. It's a survival mechanism to get you through the mayhem of childhood and adolescence with some success because—voila!—suddenly you're now an adult. However, that survival no longer serves you as an adult. In fact, that survival mode is now working against you. One of the best explanations of this is through Pete Walker and his book, *Complex PTSD: From Surviving to Thriving*. In a nutshell, he explains the basic survival paths—fight, flight, freeze—but also added another one, fawn. And that was, is, me.

I'm a fawn. And there are a lot of us. We are known as empaths, givers, and peacemakers. Now, those are not bad traits at all, unless residing behind them is fear. Fear of abandonment, rejection, humiliation, turmoil. And the playlist of scorn from childhood imbues that fear with a level of self-sacrifice that leaves us—if you too are a fawn—bewildered and wondering what the hell happened to the happy life we pictured for ourselves. We become the perfect prey for the fighters, often known for their narcissistic traits.

If you've chosen that narcissistic path, all I can say is shame on you. Of course, you already know that, since subconsciously, your life path is built on the shame of your playlist. You've bought into it to such a degree that you'll take anyone, especially those who trust you, down to the depths of your miry pit.

But if you're a fawn, or running for your life from one shiny thing to another, or paralyzed by anxiety and/or depression, then there is a way out. It's the only way out. It's high time to REBEL!

I want you to hear—read—this very carefully. I am not an expert in this. I have no PhD (though I do have my GED!), and I am not a guru. I'm not above you, nor below you. We are equally here in this excursion called life on this physical plane known as Earth. In other words, I am WITH you! I have had some extraordinary experiences, and I'm willing to share them with you because they made, and continue to make, breathtaking expansions in my life, and I am positive you can and will experience the same. BUT—

Only if you are willing to rebel. Only if you are serious about living the life you are designed to live. Experience the dreams that are of your unique Essence. Live fully and stop pretending.

Otherwise, go ahead and skip to the next chapter, or maybe even close this book altogether, lest it just be words on a page.

Alrighty then, let's go!

There is so much more I could say about that in particular here. Though the other authors might get annoyed with me if I hog all the space! But I do hope that you're excited to actually live!

One of the sensational outcomes of these discoveries is the people who are now in my life. I won't include their names here (though a bunch of them are fellow authors of this book) because listing them would, again, take up all the pages and then some. Not dim sum—then some. Though I do like a good dim sum, especially in Hong Kong!

Anyway, the people... the wondrous... no... the phenomenal... eh, too bland... the miraculous... starting to get there... people.

English, and words in general, are so limiting. It would be better if I could dance for you what I experience when I think of, or am with, the folks now in my life. They are a whole other level and energy. And I would never have known them had I not rebelled! I could not know them, because I wasn't of their same energy or frequency. This is why how you think has 100 percent to do with who shows up in your life. And until you are not just willing, but further, actually doing the thing of becoming—which begins with how you're thinking—you'll continue the same ol', same ol'. It's like pliés and tendus—the bending and straightening of knees (and there is way more to it than that), and the moving through and pointing the feet with detail—that we ballerina and danseur (male ballet dancer) types have to do on a daily basis. Sure, I can read about it in a book—oh, how funny, that's what you're doing right now! But it won't make any sense functionally until I actually do them. And it won't make me a dancer unless I do these things regularly. And I won't be a professional unless I rebuild with absolute precision these foundational pliés and tendus every single day. I have to start over each day, but bring with me what I've learned and experienced thus far. And isn't that what life is? Every day we start over. We get to leave behind what didn't work and rebuild and strengthen and find new successes. It isn't a vicious cycle after all, it's a victorious cycle! I tell you, nothing teaches life lessons quite like ballet! Ballet IS life!

Okay, I gotta come down from the ethers now! I was kind of floating there for a second, sorry! Hmm, where was I? Oh yeah! The PEOPLE! Oh, how profound are these beings and souls to me! I'm trying my best to put into words the preciousness that they are, and the richness they bring, not just to me, but to the world at large. And I either invite them into the adventure I'm experiencing, or I repel them, all with how I'm thinking. How we think, which messages we reinforce and intensify, creates who we become and how we show up. These thoughts bring people to us. Our thoughts ARE our network. They are our network, not just neurologically, but also esoterically. Knowing this, our thoughts determine the quality of the souls we bring to ourselves. Want better people around you? The greatest life proposition then is to think wisely! Not to be redundant, but think about what you're thinking!

I spent five decades letting life just happen, and I was ridiculously miserable. The one exception was my career in ballet. That was amazing and didn't just happen, or happen easily. Ballet is stratospherically competitive. And for every one of us who does make it into a professional company, there are hundreds of thousands who didn't make it but put in the same time that I did. Which, by the way, was well over 10,000 hours by the time I was 18 and had signed my first professional contract. I accomplished that not only by training and talent, but by thought and intention. It was so strong, it simply had to be. But I didn't know that that's what I was doing. I just did it! And I did it right! But I didn't know it was a thing, so I didn't know how to implement it into the rest of my life. And because I'm a fawn, I let a lot of not-so-great people shape my life. Notice I said, "let." I cannot play the victim here. Yes, there are people who did not treat me well—and that is an understatement. But I did indeed unconsciously create that. Therefore, I created the ridiculous misery that described me and my life.

If this is a really hard thing to read and a concept to digest, then you're in good company. Remember, I wanted to literally slug the guy that first revealed this thing—this Universal truth— to me. Geez, I'm so glad I didn't do that! And if you're a fawn like me, you may even feel like flogging yourself for letting this happen. I know, I just felt so stupid. But please have the oversized fawn compassion towards yourself that you typically do toward everyone else. Give yourself another chance, like you might do for someone who doesn't even deserve it.

And why don't they deserve it? Because they treat you like shit and probably will never change. There's a pattern, right? And why is it so heartbreaking and exasperating? Because you know they won't change, even though you've tried. Then again, neither have you, and that's why you're still there. It is true, the fear of change is very difficult to overcome. (But I'm hoping I haven't just described you.)

Maybe just start with something seemingly small. Keep a count on paper, or your phone somewhere, of all the negative thoughts that crop up throughout the day. This may take some practice, but continue to notice, to pay attention to, what's been playing so subtly. Turn up the volume on your soul-slaying playlist. Just know that it may be uncomfortable, or even painful, to give credence to all the nasty, putrid rhetoric you've been telling yourself since you were just a kid. We digest those words, deeds, and experiences, and they become our own words to ourselves. But they aren't even true! You ARE worthy. You ARE good enough. You ARE successful. You ARE here!

Once you start recognizing the negative chatter that's been creating your own misery, rebel against it! Refuse to believe it! It will take time for these very strong synapses to unravel, so keep at it. Don't give up! Will you fail? Well, yeah! I still do sometimes. But you can live in the victorious cycle if you choose—if you think it. So Keep. Doing. The. Work.! And pretty soon it won't be so much "work." But don't just say no to those old thoughts. Create new, life-sourced thoughts. And keep doing that every time a negative thought plays peekaboo with you. Not a cute peekaboo, but more like a menacing flea you're trying to smash, who pokes its head out over here, and then over there!

I realize this is a very simplified version of creating good thinking, but it is a start. That, and the fact that I must finish up my allotted time in this book. Just know that there are many fascinating, delightful, soul-supporting people who are more than happy to show up for you. I mean, you already have this book in your hands, with just a small sampling of these folks ready to adventure with you into a life that you may not have thought even possible. But it IS! I am proof! I am living this very thing! And to think (no pun intended), I was so very, very close to missing the life I was supposed to live. The life I wanted to live. So close to missing, well, me. Don't miss out!

Mark Brodinsky is an Emmy Award-winning TV Producer, Author, Worldwide Storyteller, Keynote Speaker, Founder of The You Matter Movement, and a two-decade-plus Health Insurance Advisor.

If his resume seems vast, it is, because Mark's mission is to positively impact the lives of One Billion people. Networking is how Mark got to where he is today. It works because everyone matters.

Connect with Mark at https://markbrodinsky.com/

CHAPTER 15

The Network Effect

"All I know is this shit works." - Mark Pallack, Harvest Investment Advisor

This shit does work, networking and more!

There I was, standing across the desk from Mark Pallack, a man I had only met a few months before. On Pallack's desk was a CD. He was explaining to me that if I were to listen to this CD from a man named Darren Hardy, and listen to Hardy's philosophy on life and his program called *Living Your Best Year Ever*, my life might change.

It was hard to believe. That is, until a day later when I slipped the CD into the player in my car (yes, I'm dating myself here), and heard Hardy say the words, "Hello, friend. I know you."

I was hooked. A networking experience was about to begin, the most profound of my life, and it continues to this day.

As the late, great Steve Jobs told us, you can't connect the dots looking forward, only looking back. That meeting and that moment happened in the spring of 2012. At that time, I needed—no, actually, I was craving—for someone to know me, because despite a pretty good family life and a fairly new job with a good company, inside, my subconscious was feeling lost.

Like something was missing. Like I was meant for more.

I come from a pretty simple background. I grew up just outside of Baltimore, Maryland, with my mom, Bonnie, my dad, Robin, and my younger sister, Donna. I attended public school and earned good grades. I didn't get into major trouble (well, for the most part—I mean, I was never in jail), and I had about half a dozen good friends.

I attended what, at the time, was called Towson State University; now it's just Towson University. In my senior year in college, I managed to gain an internship at WJZ-TV. This, after declining an internship I had already accepted at *Baltimore Magazine*. My contact at the magazine was pretty pissed when I called to tell them I was going the TV route instead. But it just felt right to me, because when I walked into the TV newsroom for the very first time, even back then, I knew I was built for more. TV was it. You've got to go with your gut.

I was right.

My local TV news career was a blast. Two months after starting my internship, the news director hired me as a writer for the 6 p.m. and 11 p.m. newscasts. It was frigging amazing. For most of my childhood, I had wanted to work in television, to actually be on TV, and this was my first step.

I was the only intern from my group of interns that they hired on to write copy.

Did I get the job by networking? Well, looking back, let's connect the dots.

Talent will take you so far, but an open heart, a helpful personality, engaging with others, and being curious about their lives will take you all the way. From the outset of my internship, I always showed up on time. I dutifully ripped scripts for each broadcast. I ran them out to the studio as needed in the middle of the news broadcast. I dressed for success. I smiled a lot. I did more than was asked of me, and I was diligent about my responsibilities.

All good.

But I also asked a ton of questions and got to know the important people around me, and whenever possible, I hung out with them after work, especially after the 11 p.m. newscast. So, either at the bar or at someone's home. I tried to be funny. I was always engaging and, most importantly, I was always interested in their lives. And I guess being handsome didn't hurt. ☺

Before I knew it, my inherent networking skills got me into a spur-of-the-moment conversation with Marty Bass. Marty was one of the weathermen, but he was also one of the most popular personalities at the TV station. He was the co-host of the *Eyewitness News* morning show, the #1-rated local morning show in Maryland and the #2 highest-rated morning news show in the entire country!

I hung out with Marty. He talked with me a lot. I asked questions, and I listened to his stories. I could tell he liked me. I went out with him socially once or twice outside the studio. That was almost 40 years ago, and Marty is still like a big brother to me.

So, several months after I graduated from college and the producer of that morning show decided he was departing at the end of the year, I was in! It wasn't even a question. Marty might have been the show's co-host, but he was the dominant force on that broadcast; he had (and still has) a big personality, and I was the one he wanted to produce that show.

If Marty thought I was the man for the producer's job—and I was—it was meant to be.

We hit it off, and for seven years, we tore that sucker up, meaning we had such a great time, got great ratings, and I even gained a nickname, The Blade (a story for another time). And so, at the end of each broadcast, I put my nickname in the middle of my producer credit: Mark "The Blade" Brodinsky.

Before I knew it, the morning show expanded. It was a 6 a.m. to 7 a.m. show, but we then added a 30-minute broadcast, called *Rise & Shine*, which aired at 5:30 a.m. I gained an on-air role, and when I was promoted as a producer to take over the 5 p.m. newscast, it opened up an opportunity for me to freelance three to four days a week in the early a.m. as a feature reporter on the morning show. I had my own segments and gained a good following.

My childhood dream—to be on TV—came true. And I networked my relationships to make my way. In 1996, I even won an Emmy Award for producing the best news broadcast in the Baltimore–Washington, D.C. Mid-Atlantic region.

Yes, I'm an Emmy winner. And I keep that sucker proudly displayed on a shelf in my basement studio. (Do a Zoom interview with me, and you'll see it in the background. ☺)

None of this would have happened in my life if I hadn't networked my way up the ladder at the TV station. Every person I met mattered. Every conversation I had mattered. I made sure I made each person I spoke with feel that they mattered.

But let's fast-forward now. Back to Mark Pallack.

After I listened to Darren Hardy's CDs and invested in the *Living Your Best Year Ever* program, I was eventually vetted and asked to join the Mastermind group that had been formed by three other people: Pallack, an investment advisor; Rob Commodari, a real estate agent; and Pete Kohlasch, a budding life coach. Then me, the health insurance agent.

It was serendipitous and one of the best moves of my life. Talk about an entry to networking.

Through Mark, Rob, and Pete, I was introduced to so many other people in other industries and other walks of life. Because of—and through—these associations, I met others who could assist me in doing things I never thought I would be able to accomplish in life, including writing and publishing my first book. Through my network, I met editors, graphic artists to assist me, and was introduced to other first-time authors who had done what I was trying to do.

I also met other people who believed fervently in the power of personal development and self-improvement, which was, after all, the foundation on which our Mastermind was built. I made acquaintance after acquaintance, and some became close friends.

My inspiration from this network of go-getters inspired me to have the courage to start a Meetup I called *Change Your Mind, Change Your Life*, sharing all the information I had gathered and wanted to share over the first five years of being immersed in personal development. I found a venue for my Meetup through someone I met while visiting a networking group, where I had been the keynote speaker one morning. The person who had the venue I needed was someone I became closer to because we did a one-to-one meeting over coffee.

Want to mix up a great brew? Start networking!

Let's face it, networking is always about people helping people.

My Meetup was well received and well attended, a big success, and I was on fire because of the energy I derived from delivering value and seeing lives changed. I launched the Meetup in 2018, having already experienced severe trauma because of the separation and pending divorce from my wife of 17 years, and missing my two teenage daughters being in my life every day. I needed to feel like part of something again, part of something bigger than myself. I wanted to feel I mattered, that I had worth and a purpose, and the Meetup and the people who attended gave me that validation.

The people who came to the Meetup—free of charge, by the way—met others with whom they could network as well. Business deals were completed, friendships were created, support was offered to those who needed it, and everyone learned something. It was amazing and proof I could create something from nothing, since, in 2017, the Meetup was just an idea in my head, and within months, it became this tangible thing that touched many, many lives.

Yes, networking matters!

And speaking of matters, how about You Matter? Perhaps the biggest networking group I've ever been a part of. I created it from scratch, once again turning "nothing" into something.

The You Matter networking movement started because of a story I heard during a Darren Hardy mentoring session (called *Darren Daily*) in August of 2019.

The story was about a woman named Cheryl, who was standing in line at a grocery store behind another woman, Sue, who was checking out.

Cheryl overheard Sue talking to the cashier about family issues. Sue said her son was in trouble and up to his old tricks, her husband had lost his job, and the family was now struggling financially. Then Cheryl saw Sue pay for her groceries with green stamps.

Cheryl, a very successful pharmaceutical executive, didn't know what to do, so in the moment, she did nothing. She could have easily paid for Sue's groceries or maybe given her husband a lead on a job. But not wanting to be presumptuous, Cheryl stayed silent.

But after Sue headed out the door, Cheryl checked out quickly and then saw Sue putting her groceries into her car in the parking lot. Cheryl went up to Sue and said, "Sorry to eavesdrop, but I heard your conversation with the cashier, and it seems like you're having a tough time right now."

Sue agreed. "It's tough, really tough right now," Sue said. At that moment, Cheryl remembered something in her purse, a card someone had given to her a few days before. Cheryl pulled out the card and handed it to Sue. Sue immediately started crying. She turned to Cheryl and said, "Oh my god. Thank you, thank you so much, you have no idea what this means to me. I haven't felt like I've had any value for a long time now."

On that card were two words: *You Matter*.

That story stopped me in my tracks. My heart started beating fast.

There I was, standing alone in my apartment, three years after my separation and a year after my divorce, on the comeback trail to feeling like I mattered, and so that tale touched me deeply. I thought to myself, "Self, why don't you have cards made? Why don't you hand them out, just like Cheryl did?"

So, I immediately called my girlfriend, Stephanie, who, fortunately for me, was the salesperson and administrative manager for a small, local printing company. I told her I heard this story about this You Matter card, and I wanted to have my own made. Later that day, I shared my vision for the card. I wanted it to be business-card size and have a red background with white letters spelling out the words *You Matter*. And I wanted the letters on the card to be raised, so not only would the person who received the card read the message, but if they closed their eyes and ran their fingers along the words *You Matter*, they could "feel" it too. Stephanie joked, "All these people you want to give cards to, are they blind? It's not braille." I said, "No, it's just another tactile way for people to feel their worth and value."

On the back of the card was the mission I felt whispered to me about five years before this moment. "I am now positively impacting the lives of a billion people." Underneath that message was my name. That's it. I wasn't selling anything to anyone, just sharing what existed in my heart and soul.

That's how you start a network. A common theme, a common idea, a common purpose. I knew I was about to build the most meaningful network the world has ever known.

Why would I do this, you ask? Well, see if this statement resonates with you as a human being. It comes from psychologist and philosopher William James: "The deepest principle in human nature is the craving to be appreciated."

That's it. Full stop. End of sentence. Game over.

Feeling that *You Matter* is not just a wish or a desire; it's a craving. It's as vital to our survival as humans as food, water, and shelter. Without the first three, you will physically die. Without the fourth, feeling you have worth and a purpose, you die inside, and that's a long, slow, painful death.

And this is where my soul speaks to humanity. This network of humanity. We are all part of this universe. Break that down into "uni"—meaning one—and "verse"—as in song. This one song.

This network of human beings. If I can get one billion people to believe they matter on a daily basis, the ripple effect of tossing that pebble in the ocean can touch all 8 billion people on the planet.

For more than six years now, I've handed out these cards at random, mainly to people I meet who provide me with any service, or someone I'm engaged in conversation with, because I know they need it. They don't just need it, they crave it. And it doesn't mean they are showing any signs of a lack of worth. As a matter of fact, the people who seem to have it all together are often the ones carrying the heaviest burden. Maybe they are hiding what is really going on inside.

The bottom line is, you don't know what you don't know. So, how can you judge what the person you are meeting really needs in the moment?

Words matter. Energy matters. Giving matters.

This *You Matter* networking is not self-promotion; it's collaboration, it's people building, it's a meaningful human connection. It's not being an influencer, it's being a lighthouse. I'm not trying to be a guru, I'm simply a mirror.

Think of how you'd feel in the moment if someone handed you a card with those two words on it: *You Matter*. Would it make you feel a certain way? Would it encourage you to love yourself? Would you want to be part of a group where people are living this feeling each day?

I live this feeling because I never leave the house without *You Matter* cards in my pocket. When someone receives a card, you can see it reflected in their heart and soul; there's your mirror! A smile, a look, sometimes tears, sometimes clutching the card to their heart. Often I hear, "Thank you so much. This is great. This is special." Or, "Thank you. I needed this today!"

And so I know this is the greatest networking of my life. My why, my how, my heart, my soul. You can say it's a movement, not a network. I would beg to differ. Networking is the process of building connections and relationships. Look it up. That is what I'm attempting to do here.

At first, there were just the cards. Now there's a *You Matter* book, there's a *You Matter* song, there are daily *You Matter Minutes*, there's *You Matter* Storytelling, there's *You Matter* coaching, and there's *You Matter* swag.

Nowadays, my card has a QR code on the back which links people to my *You Matter* website, where they can see pictures of people holding up the cards and connect with all the things I mentioned above, and connect with one another. We're building a worldwide community. We're networking for a higher purpose. We're building a world where people believe in and love themselves. Because when you love you, the world beats a path to your door. When you don't love yourself first, how can you expect another person to love you as well?

The network effect is in motion here and has been for some time now. It's not focused on only business networking; however, the people I am introduced to because of this *You Matter* movement are now part of my network and an advisor team as I build out this business model as well.

You don't always have to join an established networking group, though that works great as well—just like Ken Walls' GrowLive Academy. ☺ But the reason I want to join a group like that is because I believe I can bring value to others. The goal is to give without the expectation of anything in return.

Giving is the key. To do all I can with all I have been given.

The networking effect is real. It's necessary. It's what makes life richer. You are the product of the four or five people you spend the most time with; where they're going, you're going. And those people can introduce you to four or five more very meaningful and worthwhile relationships.

We are all part of this social tribe of humans, and we all need one another. There is no shortcut to this. We can't do life alone. We are in a constant state of flow, and that flow should pass from one human being to another. A rising tide lifts all boats.

Network and see life expand. See growth amplified. Realize that other people want to help you. Deep inside, everyone wants to help another person. You can't escape what it means to be human.

You are a miracle. A masterpiece. A hero. Don't cheat the world of your gifts and talents and the very reason you are here.

God wants you to network. He wants you to share your value. He made you unique for a reason.

So dive into networking and start swimming. The effect it will have on your life will take you to distant shores, other worlds, and make your life as good as it can be!

After all, isn't that what we're all after? Enjoy the journey. It's not about the destination, so take the path with those who help you feel that you matter.

You do, and networking is the key!

You Matter!

Mark Brodinsky

Strategic, crisis, corporate and political communications expert Kay Daly has nearly four decades of experience. From Hollywood to Washington DC and beyond, Kay has been a sought after TV, radio, podcast and print

interview, media coach, columnist, speechwriter and consultant. She is the host of "The Daly Fix" livestream/podcast and a popular X spaces host.

Dubbed "the next Phyllis Schlafly" by ACU Chairman David Keene, Kay's grassroots activism and coalition building on behalf of Bush 43's judicial nominees earned Kay the "Ronald Reagan Award" from CPAC, the "Distinguished Service Award" from the Senate Republican Conference, and an invitation to testify at a House Judiciary Committee hearing from Chairman Jim Sensenbrenner. In an attempt to buttress the DOJ Special Counsel's partisan lawfare against the Senate Judiciary Committee Republicans' Nominations Counsel [Manuel Miranda], Sen. Dick Durbin probed Kay's meetings at the White House by asking Court of Appeals nominee Brett Kavanaugh, "Do you know Kay R. Daly?" When Alberto Gonzales was rumored to be on Bush's short list to replace Sandra Day O'Connor, The Washington Times quoted Kay declaring his potential nomination to be dead on arrival because "Gonzales is Spanish for Souter." In a Congressional primary during the Obama era, Kay was endorsed by Sean Hannity, Mark Levin, James Dobson, Bo Snerdley, and David Bossie. A former staffer or campaign advisor to Gov. Pete Wilson, Sen. Phil Gramm, Reagan Administration official Tex Lezar, and Sen. Fred Thompson, Kay was the NCGOP Communications Director and an Authorized Broadcast Media Surrogate for President Trump's 2016 campaign.

CHAPTER 16

The Power Grid: Navigating Networking in the Political Swamp

Sitting at a stoplight at the corner of 15th Street and Pennsylvania Avenue, next to the U.S. Treasury Department in Washington, D.C., I watched with amusement as the motorcycle police officers came screaming up to the intersection to blockade traffic. Suddenly, the Presidential motorcade, always impressive to behold, sped by on its way to the White House complex.

It was State of the Union night, and I had just come from the White House itself to watch the speech and attend a brief reception. Never did it become routine to visit the White House—be it for a meeting at the Old Executive Office Building, or certainly for State of the Union night. It's a pinch-yourself moment to meander through the East Room or the Blue Room, rubbing elbows with famous political folks.

Watching vehicle after vehicle pass by, it struck me what a surreal existence I enjoy. The President of the United States had just delivered a major address—not just to the nation but to the world. A speech that contained a line I helped to craft. A speech I had just watched from the White House.

How in the world did I get to this moment?

It was a bizarre combination of hard work, pure dumb luck, recognizing opportunities as they arose, and, most importantly, strategic networking.

The networking side of the political world can seem straightforward, but in truth, it can be a minefield if done haphazardly. Being aware of the goal, the individuals involved, agenda awareness, timing, and messaging can be critical elements to achieving success.

So let's go back to the beginning. It was successful, yet simple networking that radically changed the direction of my life, and certainly my career path.

It was 1986, and I was dating someone my mother just couldn't stand. So what does a good Southern mother do? Why, send her daughter away, of course! I had already had internships in Hollywood and other opportunities along the way, but nothing had truly felt like I had found my actual calling.

Then my mother picked up the phone and called one of her close friends. Within moments, she arranged a summer internship in Washington, D.C., with then U.S. Senator Pete Wilson (R-CA). Within days of landing, I had caught a wicked case of Potomac fever.

Washington seemed to be the center of the universe, where news was constantly breaking. The sense of history was palpable, and the buildings, the monuments, and the museums were delightful to explore. One day, while strolling past the Capitol, a friend who had logged far more time inside the Beltway gave me some of the best advice. He saw that I was staring appreciatively at the beautiful Capitol dome against a clear blue sky. He told me that the moment I glanced at the dome and didn't catch my breath or get that chill, it would be time to leave Washington. Burnout is real.

The journey of developing networking strategies started early on. I had lucked into a terrific first boss/mentor. The communications director for the Senator asked me one day what career path I wanted to take. I told him, unflinchingly and with the boldness of youth, that I wanted his job. He chuckled and then seriously let me know that not many women were communications directors. I immediately retorted that Mary Matalin seemed to be doing great at the RNC.

At that moment, I wasn't sure if he had decided I had overstepped, but he began to take me along to press conferences, hearings, events of all kinds. I observed closely as he worked a room—be it full of press, staff, whoever. Business cards were the currency of the realm, and not only did he bring a stack with him, but I noted that every card he received, he would make a quick note on the back of the card about the discussion or request he had encountered. And he followed up on every request without fail.

Must have done something right, because they asked me to work on both the Senate campaign and the Gubernatorial campaign that immediately followed. Yet another mentor entered my life who gave me a mantra I have embraced for the whole of my career. He said, "Kay, people have to be able to count on you."

So, armed with a stack of notated business cards and burgeoning rolodexes, I dove in fully to better understand the power of developing effective networks. The collection of contacts is barely scratching the surface of successful networking.

In any project you undertake in politics, the first step is to determine the goal. Make it manageable and realistic. Whether it is making a career move and seeking out a new job, building a coalition to support legislation or policy effort, or creating a target list for messaging, media, or any other strategic communications effort, develop your networking lists based upon total focus on the goal.

If obtaining a job in the D.C. political world is the goal, decide which sector would meet your skill set and experience. Capitol Hill has actual employment offices in both the House and the Senate. But there are other sources as well that include email listings, résumé banks, and, most of all, word of mouth. The best job opportunities are usually snapped up before they even reach public disclosure in any kind of advertising mechanism.

That's right! Know your Rolodex contacts well enough to understand who would be ideal to approach. Have a list of questions prepared, and ask your contacts what they have heard in terms of employment opportunities. Ask for their best advice. Should they know of a potential position, ask if they know whom to contact to start the interview process. Ask if it is acceptable to mention their name to the key contact.

Rinse and repeat.

It is critical not to make contact only when you are asking for a favor. That's the way to alienate particularly well-positioned contacts who get many such requests all too frequently. And always thank your contacts for their assistance, advice, and friendship.

Taking notes as you chat with your contacts about family details, birthdays, work promotions, etc., is incredibly important. Don't make every conversation completely about you and your agenda. And if you land the job thanks to one of your contacts, if you really want to make an impression, hand-write a thank-you note. Yes, for snail mail. It shows humility, gratitude, and thoughtfulness. It is a lost art and will set you apart in a memorable way.

Finding the career path after college in Washington and beyond worked exactly through this effort. At first, it was more trial and error, but with each successive opportunity, it became easier to focus on those contacts who would be well-positioned (and hopefully willing) to assist in achieving the goal.

Having employers who are also mentors, or others in your constellation who are mentors to you, also opens networking opportunities quite often. Meeting key contacts via a mentor usually yields far better results than meeting someone cold. Even a mutual friend, not necessarily a mentor, can give you a virtual stamp of approval that is harder to obtain without such an introduction.

Not that such a situation is required, but it is optimal. That does not preclude the importance of meeting someone out of the blue and adding them to the old Rolodex.

After graduation day from UCSD, while my fellow graduates were enjoying European tours, I packed a suitcase and tossed a stack of résumés in for good measure. I told my parents I wanted to visit friends in Washington, D.C., but left out the job-hunting part of the plan.

Within days of arrival, I secured some very worthwhile interviews, both by word of mouth and via the job placement offices on Capitol Hill. Many young, earnest females would be placed in scheduling or some other administrative position. But the combination of press office experience, time spent on Capitol Hill, plus campaign hours on my résumé, opened the door to more options.

In what would be one of those pivotal moments in my career, while interviewing with the Projects Office Director for Senator Phil Gramm (R-TX), I was told that my résumé was impressive, but it was just a shame that I had no Texas ties.

Immediately, I thought, Now hold on there, pardner. Although I had been born in Los Angeles, my mother was a fifth-generation

Texan. And to get the California out of me, my mother wisely made sure I spent plenty of time with family located throughout the state. All of which I expressed to my interviewer, who smiled and asked me when I could start.

There were three of us who worked for the Projects Office Director. Two of us split all the executive branch's departments and agencies as our areas of responsibility. The third worked on federal judge, U.S. Marshals, and U.S. Attorney office nominations.

It was a PhD-level education in terms of observing firsthand the process of how our leviathan, bloated government operates.

My job was to work with mayors, county judges, CEOs, university presidents, local schools, housing directors, small businesses, NASA, local, state, and federal elected officials, among so many others, to find grants, push line-item appropriations for worthy projects, and announce successes working with the Senator's press office.

In addition, whenever the Senator went back to the state—which was often—I would contribute a substantial amount of information in briefing papers that the Senator would review before any event.

My writing improved, my knowledge of strategic communications tactics, appropriations, executive branch, and legislative processes grew exponentially, and my rolodex exploded.

I also learned management tactics from one of the best Chiefs of Staff on Capitol Hill. She was one of the very rare female chiefs on the Hill and had been with the Senator since his days as an economics professor at Texas A&M. She was petite, but a powerhouse of focus, encyclopedic knowledge, and grit, with a dash of Southern charm. This was a Chief of Staff who could tell you "no" with a quiet firmness that would induce you to apologize for asking in the first place.

Her superpower was not in being cold or unpleasant, but instead an efficient resolve to ensure the principal was effectively supported and protected, all the while graciously serving the citizens of the great state of Texas. And everyone on staff was aligned with that agenda.

Networking led to the next career opportunity in the private sector, where I focused on law enforcement issues across the nation, particularly in the realm of that new technology folks were calling "the internet." And yes, my Rolodex continued to grow rapidly.

Which led to another critical crossroads in my career.

At the suggestion of several of my Texas law enforcement clients, I flew to Dallas and met Tex Lezar. Tex, a graduate of Yale and the UT Austin Law School, where he was the Editor-in-Chief of the law review, had served in President Ronald Reagan's Department of Justice as Chief of Staff to the Attorney General. He was also appointed to be the Assistant Attorney General for the Office of Legal Policy. Early in his career, Tex worked for William F. Buckley, Jr., and as a speechwriter for President Richard Nixon.

Lezar's extraordinarily talented wife had transformed the White House Media Relations office in the Reagan Administration and, upon their return to Texas, started a very successful strategic communications firm that specialized in both crisis communications and media training. I learned so much and met more wonderful, talented people than I can mention. It was a surreal opportunity on any given day, whether I attended the Richard Nixon funeral or enjoyed a sandwich lunch with then–NYC Mayor Rudy Giuliani at City Hall.

As Chief of Staff, I made sure Tex's columns and radio/TV hits happened and went well. He was the author of *Making Government Work: A Conservative Agenda for the States*, and President Reagan penned the foreword. Tex updated the book, and I helped in the editing process. All the living former Republican Presidents gave jacket quotes, and each chapter was written by a leading expert in a variety of policy arenas.

Tex was also a founder and President of the Texas Public Policy Foundation, part of a growing movement of conservative state think tanks across the nation. One of the most rewarding projects was the establishment of a school choice voucher program in three key Texas cities. And he ran for Lt. Governor on the same ticket as his Yale classmate George W. Bush.

Each of these projects deepened my knowledge and experience base, plus multiplied those key contacts across the nation. By this point, I was meeting former Presidents, Senators, Congressmen, Governors, and some of the most accomplished political writers, thinkers, activists, and leaders.

In terms of a political earthquake, 1994 in the House of Representatives was the place to be as a conservative. Newt Gingrich had orchestrated a seismic victory not seen in the previous 40 years when he won the majority in the House. I was asked to join the staff of a freshman member from North Carolina as the press secretary.

Learning and absorbing from Speaker Gingrich, whose knowledge of history, policy, and politics is virtually unmatched, was rocket fuel. Add to that a growing circle of brilliant, innovative political allies and friends, and life was never dull.

Several staffers from key leadership offices would meet regularly in the Capitol in what's known as the Crow's Nest. It was a cigar aficionado group with plenty of brainstorming, information exchanging, and loads of laughs as well.

I had never smoked a cigar in my life.

But this group was far too important to let a little thing like that stand in my way! So learn about cigars, I most certainly did. And the networking was worth however many years those cigars took off my life.

These networking opportunities led to more invitations to more exclusive events and meetings. I viewed networking as a pathway and worked very hard not to abuse the contacts or relationships I had been blessed to make. My policy was, and still is, to only make an ask when necessary and be responsive to an ask made of me.

Moving down to North Carolina at the request of my boss led to the greatest adventure yet. I met a young Chapel Hill law student who was handsome, brilliant, hilarious, and truly kind-hearted. Make no mistake, I won the husband lottery. He has been an extraordinary father, provider, and partner for 29 years.

There was a series of career opportunities that broadened the knowledge bank and the rolodex. By this time, my clients and projects included Fortune 500 companies, Hollywood stars and producers, and a wide variety of political organizations, leaders, political party leadership, and elected officials.

Reputation management wasn't only for my clients, however. Having observed extraordinarily talented individuals make critical errors due to one or more thoughtless faux pas taught me the key lesson that credibility is earned by the teaspoon and lost by the wheelbarrow full.

Egos are a huge component of the political arena. But if the lesson is never learned that no one is indispensable and everyone is replaceable, self-reflection is absent and, eventually, a shiny reputation is gone too. Competition can be healthy, but only when assessing one's own faults or failures honestly and realistically. To only look askance at someone who succeeded where you failed, rather than doing an internal review of where you could have improved, can be a fatal flaw.

Having learned some of these key maxims was essential to the next chapter of my career.

We decided to move back up to Washington, D.C. My husband had worked in the political realm for years and, right before we moved, had been an attorney on the Bush v. Gore recount team. We also learned I was pregnant with our first child.

Upon arrival, I was asked to put together a plan to support John Ashcroft, nominated to be U.S. Attorney General.

It struck me that the hallmark of our confirmation battles had been a defensive posture of fear. And we were far more concerned with what we were saying rather than what was being heard, while broad-brushing messaging based upon largely false assumptions about target audiences.

Job one was to go on offense. Now, back in the day, it was never advised to schedule a press conference on a Monday.

But that's precisely what I did.

And I burned up the phone lines calling grassroots organizations, policy experts, key legal eagles, and well-recognized opinion leaders. It was a massive success. For the rest of the week, leftists were the ones on defense for once, unused to any aggressive posture from conservatives, usually terrified of any hint of a negative headline or a raised eyebrow for deviating even slightly from the norm.

A center-right coalition was born.

It turned out to be a watershed moment. I had an inkling that it was significant and even mentioned it to a colleague as we walked to our cars post–press conference. But the full impact did not hit me until three extraordinary women approached me about formalizing the coalition and working to confirm constitutional originalists to the all-important federal bench.

Hindsight truly is 20/20. Realizing that I had just been invited to the White House to meet with key staff, as well as staff members from Senate leadership and the Senate Judiciary Committee, I pushed aside any objections I might have had to taking on this mammoth project while no less than seven months pregnant.

The primary priority was the plan. There had to be an education phase about the importance of federal courts in every American's life. Messaging outside of Washington, D.C., and the legal eagle community had to be impactful and relevant. Most Americans didn't know the difference between a federal court and a traffic court, but they had some notion that courts in general were where bad things could happen. Knowing that federal judgeships are lifetime appointments demonstrated the urgency of putting the best, most qualified nominees on the bench.

Federal judges should apply the Constitution as it is written, not as they would like it to be.

Federal courts take on a very wide range of policy questions. Networking was key to the organization of this effort. Grassroots organizations throughout the nation all have policy agendas and are subject-matter experts. If there was a need to find an organization that focused on a particular subject, we would ask coalition members to rifle through their rolodexes to fill the need.

Depending on the issue, we could move legal eagles into position to shore up the legal community. Internal D.C. communication efforts were handled very specifically, depending on subject and venue. And proactively, creativity was the name of the game and would be assigned to one or more organizations. If issues arose, it would just be another layer to the messaging.

The intriguing part of this effort was the seamless way organizations that may have never worked together, or worse, might be diametrically opposed in several issue areas, still managed to agree and put aside differences, given the critical goals that had been set. Because I was not affiliated with a large organization, I was viewed as an honest broker and non-threatening to any coalition organization's agenda. Many doubted we would be successful. And there certainly were roadblocks along the way. But we grew in numbers and with demonstrable successes.

I found myself in the surreal position of attending meetings at the White House or Senate leadership offices frequently. At these meetings, I brought my infant son, Patrick, who charmed attendees and would flirt outrageously with any pretty lady who caught his eye. The coalition took to calling him "POTUS."

While pregnant with Daly child number two, it was an honor of a lifetime at CPAC to win the Reagan Award. It is given to the usually unsung grassroots heroes of the conservative movement who have made a massive impact. It was not my award alone but the extraordinary work of the coalition that created the numerous successes, and I said as much at the podium that night. I will be eternally grateful to each coalition participant for their passion, insight, advice, brilliance, and friendship.

Meanwhile, my husband was a counsel on the Senate Judiciary Committee, which led to executive branch jobs and Chief of

Staff opportunities with members of Congress. And he has since gone on to become the leading digital marketing fundraiser for President Trump, party organizations, hundreds of candidates, and many grassroots groups. We complemented each other's skill sets and effectively doubled the networking ground we could cover.

I took my strategic communications toolkit, combined with the experience and advice of amazing mentors and friends, along with a hefty Rolodex, and applied those learned skills to a wide variety of projects and campaigns in the years that followed. But looking back at that remarkable night, sitting at the traffic light a stone's throw from the White House and watching the Presidential motorcade speed by the front bumper of my car, having just attended a State of the Union watch party at the White House, I was filled with hope.

It is a rare thing in politics to enjoy real change because of the very design the founding fathers established. The tension between opposing ideas or candidates breeds a "two steps forward, three steps back" situation time and time again.

To witness the historic decisions made, particularly by the Supreme Court, was something I never believed I would see in my lifetime. To still hear echoes of the message points I had penned long ago is remarkable. But it is the absolute truth that one person can change the world.

Well, one person and a remarkable network of talented, brilliant individuals.

Lonnie Wills is a U.S. Marine Corps veteran, technology leader, and executive with a track record of building high-impact businesses and teams.

After decades in the private sector leading Fortune 100 projects and launching successful startups, he now serves as the Executive Director of the Jerry Ambrose Veterans Council, working to improve the lives of veterans across Arizona.

A former U.S. Senate candidate, Lonnie continues to advocate for principled leadership, community service, and veteran support. His career is built on grit, integrity, and the power of strong relationships.

CHAPTER 17
Introduction - Who I Am & Why This Matters

I didn't grow up with a head start. What I had was a broom, a pair of work boots, and a dad who believed in teaching by doing.

It was 1977 — the middle of a recession — and I was seven years old. My dad had just started his own handyman business, Mike's Handyman Service. While most kids my age were still figuring out cartoons, I was figuring out how to sweep up sawdust and keep a job site clean. My first official title? Cleanup crew. I ran the broom. And I ran it well.

That was my introduction to work ethic — not from a book, but from Saturdays spent hauling trash, sweeping floors, and learning what it meant to take pride in even the smallest task. My dad didn't just build homes — he built me. Every weekend, I was by his side learning how to frame, paint, fix, and finish. But more importantly, I was learning how to *show up* — with effort, consistency, and integrity.

Around that same time, I'd spend my summers at my grandparents' place during berry season. That's when I connected the dots: the more berries I picked, the more money I made. And the more money I made, the more freedom I had to buy what I wanted. Simple, powerful economics for a kid still under four feet tall.

By third grade, I had my own lawn mowing business. I kept it running through sixth grade, when I took on a paper route that included one of the steepest hills in town. Every morning, rain or shine, I hit that route on my bike, stopping at each door to place the paper on a hook. That job taught me service, discipline, and the value of being dependable. I still remember the $50 tips at Christmas — not because of the money, but because it meant I had done the job right.

I played soccer year-round from the time I was seven, coached by my dad. Our team placed second in the state championships twice. Sports taught me about leadership and resilience, but more than anything, they taught me that you don't win alone. You win with a team.

Those lessons carried into the Marine Corps, into every business I've started, and into the relationships that have shaped my life. Today, I run an AI company — CallAssistant.ai — helping businesses connect better. But tech is just a tool. The real magic is in the people.

In this chapter, I want to show you what real connection looks like — not the kind you collect at networking mixers, but the kind you build brick by brick, handshake by handshake. Because if you ask me what changed my life? It wasn't luck. It was the people I met along the way.

2. The Moments That Changed Everything

People talk about overnight success like it's real. It's not. For me, it was a series of small wins, stacked over time, each one building momentum — and each one fueled by a connection, a conversation, or a challenge I didn't back down from.

One of those early sparks happened in 10th grade. I had already been knee-deep in electronics — fascinated by how things worked and how to build them. That's when I built my first robot.

It wasn't just motors and gears; I wrote software on a Commodore 64 that interfaced with the robot directly. I developed a "learning mode" so I could control the robot with a joystick, record the steps in memory, and then replay the entire sequence with perfect accuracy. Today, we call that automation. In 1985, I just called it a fun challenge.

That robot taught me something huge: **technology wasn't just something to use — it was something I could create.**

Around that time, I joined VICA — the Vocational Industrial Clubs of America. It wasn't just about electronics. I competed in resume writing, job interviews, and extemporaneous speaking. It was about becoming well-rounded, knowing how to present yourself, lead a team, and show up with confidence.

In my senior year, I became the **State President of VICA for Washington State.** That wasn't just a title — it was a turning point. I was leading students across the state, speaking at conferences, managing events, and representing the future of the skilled trades. That role gave me my first taste of real leadership. It also opened doors — to mentors, professionals, and opportunities that wouldn't have existed otherwise.

One mentor in particular pulled me aside after a speech and said, "You have the ability to move people. Use it wisely." That stuck with me. Because at the end of the day, all the tech in the world doesn't matter if you can't connect with your team, your customers, your audience.

Those experiences laid the foundation for everything that came next: joining the Marine Corps, building companies, leading teams, and eventually founding CallAssistant.ai. But it all started with wiring circuits on a kitchen table, coding on an old keyboard, and being surrounded by people who pushed me to be more.

If there was a single thread running through all of it, it's this: **your life can change when someone sees potential in you and says, "Let's go."**

Sometimes it's a coach. Sometimes it's a customer. Sometimes it's a mentor who sees the spark before you even know what to do with it. Those moments — and those people — are the real network effect. They're not chance. They're catalysts.

3. Networking Isn't a Numbers Game

Most people think networking is about collecting business cards or adding people on LinkedIn. They treat it like a game of volume — the more names, the more leverage. But let me tell you something: **your network doesn't grow because of how many people you know — it grows based on how many people trust you.**

When I joined the Marine Corps, I entered the reserves. My dad had served in Vietnam — spent nine months in-country — and I was born while he was still overseas. That legacy mattered to me. I wanted to serve, but I also had plans to get an engineering degree. My parents always told me college was important, but they also told me something else: **"If you want it, you're going to have to earn it."** So I did.

While going to school for mechanical engineering, I landed a job with an engineering firm — and that opened up my first real door. Because of my background in computing and electronics, I got a shot at managing their network systems. That job led to the next: running a Banyan VINES and Novell network for another company. Then came the call from IBM.

They were launching a new group called TSS, and I became a Microsoft Certified Network Engineer and data sniffer expert. When American Express had a massive network issue, I was the one flown in to fix it. From there, my name got around. I became a go-to guy. Not because I knew everything — but because people knew they could rely on me to figure it out.

When TSS merged back into IBM, the relationships I had built inside that team stayed intact. That mattered later. I became a first-line manager, leading teams across multiple states. Our biggest project? A $14 billion outsourcing effort with Washington Mutual, converting acquired banks into WaMu branches across the West Coast. High stakes, high visibility — and once again, **relationships were the glue.**

At the end of 1999, I left IBM, cashed in my 401(k), and launched my first business. I had one goal: **be the CEO of my own company by the time I was 30.** I hit that goal, but not without scars.

I brought in people I trusted — one was my former boss from the engineering firm. Another was someone I worked with at Lucent Technologies. We started building the MSN network, which was being managed at the time by Enron Broadband. You probably know how that story ends.

Enron went under, and I was left holding $250,000 in unpaid invoices. My credit line was $1 million. I took a second mortgage on my house just to make payroll in November and December. And when the bank called my note, I couldn't cover it. No cash flow. No work. I had to let my entire team go. It took me two more years and selling my house to climb out of that hole. I never recovered the money. The best offer I got from the Enron bankruptcy was ten cents on the dollar. I was insulted. Meanwhile, the execs who helped destroy the company floated away with golden parachutes.

But even then — even in failure — my network didn't abandon me. One of the investors from my first company called me and said, "I want you to meet someone." That someone was Jim Johnson, a CEO in San Diego. He asked me to come on board as CIO of his public company. Another door. Another relationship. Another chance.

That role brought me into the world of Salesforce — first as a customer, then as a believer. I started my second company, **CloudTrigger**, with zero dollars and built it into one of Salesforce's top five consulting partners in the world. Not because I had a big marketing budget. Because I had a strong reputation — and a network that believed in me.

I sold CloudTrigger in 2012 and went on to lead **G2 Technologies** for 13 years. I kept building — and more importantly, I kept connecting. Every major opportunity I've had has come through a relationship. That's what brought me to **CallAssistant.ai**, where we took an idea and grew it into a platform with over 100,000 users in just a few years.

The lesson? **Your network is your equity.** Not in a transactional sense — in a human sense. People invest in people they trust. They follow people who show up. And they open doors for people who deliver.

That's why networking isn't a numbers game. It's a character game.

4. How to Build Real Connections That Last

The biggest misconception people have about networking is that it's something you *do* — like a task you check off your to-do list. But for me, networking has never been transactional. It's not a pitch. It's not a coffee meeting. It's not a business card exchange. It's a lifestyle.

If you want to build real, lasting connections, you have to **stop chasing people and start showing up for them.**

That mindset started with my dad. When I was a kid, we didn't call it networking — we called it being a good neighbor. We did great work, and we did it with integrity. If someone's faucet was leaking or their fence was falling down, my dad didn't need a marketing campaign. His name got around because people *trusted* him.

That stuck with me.

Every job, every project, every opportunity I've had came from relationships I built by doing three things: **adding value, staying consistent, and doing what I said I would do.** That's it.

You'd be surprised how rare that is.

Show Up Early, Stay Late, Deliver More

When I was managing projects at IBM or leading massive network cutovers, I wasn't just the guy who got things done — I was the guy who understood the entire stack, from the cabling to the protocol layers. I worked hard to master my subject matter. I didn't walk into a room trying to prove I was the smartest — but more often than not, someone else would say it.

That reputation didn't come from luck or credentials. It came from **hours of research, relentless problem-solving, and a mindset of constant learning.** I became an expert because I made it my mission to understand the full picture — not just my piece of it.

People trusted me not just because I delivered results, but because they knew I'd already done the work behind the scenes to make sure it was right. That's how you earn trust. That's how you build credibility. And in turn, that's how relationships form — because people want to work with people who are *prepared.*

Give First — Without Keeping Score

One of the things that's served me well in business is the habit of **giving first.** Not just favors, not just intros — but time, attention, ideas. Whether I was mentoring someone trying to break into the tech space, helping a former teammate land a role, or offering real talk to a founder in over his head — I never made it about what I'd get back.

Most people won't remember what you said. But they *will* remember how you showed up when they needed you.

And guess what? Those moments come back around.

The investor who connected me to a public company's CEO? That came from a relationship I built years earlier — just by being dependable. The colleague who joined my startup and helped scale it? That came from shared history and trust, not a job posting.

Stay in the Game Long Enough to Matter

Real relationships don't form overnight. They're built over time. You've got to stay in the game long enough for people to see your character — not just your resume.

The reason my phone still rings is that I didn't vanish after a win, and I didn't disappear after a loss. I stayed in the trenches. I owned my failures. I lifted others up. And I kept investing in the people who were investing in me.

Sometimes that meant a call just to check in. Sometimes it meant flying across the country to help close a deal. Other times, it meant showing up for someone who couldn't do anything for me in return.

That's the long game. That's the difference.

Never Burn Bridges — Even When You Want To

Let me be real for a second. Not every relationship in business is rosy. I've been burned. I've been betrayed. I've watched people I trusted turn opportunistic when money hits the table.

But here's what I learned: **you don't need to burn a bridge to walk away from it.**

You can hold the line without throwing gasoline. You can preserve your reputation without sacrificing your boundaries. And sometimes, the quiet exit is louder than the dramatic one — because people are always watching how you handle the hard stuff.

Grace under pressure creates long-term respect. And in the business world, that's a currency that never loses value.

Keep It Human

Technology has changed everything — how we work, how we meet people, how we build companies. But no amount of AI, automation, or social media will ever replace **human connection**.

People want to feel seen. They want to know you're listening. They want to believe that when you reach out, it's not just because you want something.

That's why I still send texts to check in. That's why I jump on calls when I don't have to. That's why I say yes to speaking with a young founder who's just trying to figure it all out.

Because someone once did that for me.

And that's how you build a network that lasts — one real connection at a time.

5. Leveraging Your Network Without Exploiting It

If you're going to build a strong network, you also need to know **how to use it — without abusing it**. That's where a lot of people go wrong.

Some folks treat networking like a favor bank. They think relationships are just transactions: "I did something for you, now you owe me." That mindset might get you a couple of short-term wins — but it'll kill your long game.

You don't leverage relationships by pulling on them like a rope. You leverage them by creating momentum together.

Throughout my career, I've leaned on my network — but not with entitlement. I reached out with a clear purpose, respect for their time, and a track record that made people want to say yes.

When I left IBM and started my first company, the people who came with me didn't do it because I promised them equity or sold them a dream. They did it because they *knew me*. They'd seen me in action. They knew I wouldn't flinch in a crisis. And they knew that if we won, we'd win together.

When I needed a partner to help run operations, I called someone I worked with at Lucent Technologies. He didn't hesitate. Not because of a pitch — because of a relationship.

The Rule: Create Value Before You Ever Make an Ask

If you want to be able to lean on your network, you've got to earn that trust *long before* you need it.

That means you show up when it's inconvenient. You help when it doesn't benefit you. You remember the birthdays. You celebrate their wins. You listen more than you talk. You treat people like humans, not opportunities.

When you do that, you don't have to pitch when the time comes. You just call. And more often than not, they answer with: "How can I help?"

That's the difference between a cold ask and a trusted referral. One comes from hustle. The other comes from **reputation**.

Don't Weaponize Your Rolodex

Over the years, I've watched people get access to powerful networks — and then burn through them by using connections like ammunition. They drop names, over-promise, under-deliver, or worse — they play people against each other. That's not leveraging. That's manipulation.

I've had to walk away from partnerships where people were chasing the shortcut, not the solution. And I've seen how fast doors close when people feel used.

The most valuable thing in your network isn't your contact list — it's your *character*. That's what people remember when your name comes up in a room you're not in.

Make the Right Ask, the Right Way

If you've done the work, you'll know when the timing is right to reach out. But even then, there's an art to the ask.

Here's my rule: when I reach out to someone in my network, I'm always clear, direct, and low-pressure. I let them know why I thought of them, what I'm working on, and how they can *opt in* — not feel obligated.

The best relationships aren't built on guilt. They're built on mutual respect.

And sometimes, leveraging your network isn't about asking for anything at all. It's about creating something valuable *and inviting your network to be a part of it*.

That's what I did with CloudTrigger. That's what we're doing now at CallAssistant. People don't just show up because of me — they show up because they believe in the mission, and they know I'll deliver.

The Bottom Line

Your network is a living, breathing thing. You can grow it, nurture it, and yes, leverage it — but only if you treat it with respect.

People aren't stepping stones. They're partners, collaborators, and often the difference between a door opening or staying shut.

So use your network. But never forget the most important part: **don't use people.**

6. The Future of Networking

Technology is changing everything — from how we communicate, to how we connect, to how we do business. We've gone from handshakes to Zoom calls, from business cards to DMs, and now we're entering a world where AI is doing the talking *before* we even pick up the phone.

But here's the truth: **the future of networking won't be built by algorithms. It'll be built by people who know how to stay human in a digital world.**

I've seen it firsthand. At CallAssistant.ai, we're using artificial intelligence to make conversations more efficient — answering phones, qualifying leads, scheduling appointments — all without losing the personal touch. But that only works when the technology **supports the relationship**, not replaces it.

There's a danger in thinking that tools are the connection. They're not. They're just the delivery system.

In the coming years, we'll see more automation, more avatars, and more AI-powered communication. That's fine. But don't forget this: **authenticity will always outperform automation when it comes to trust.**

The business world will get faster, but trust will still take time. Digital tools will make outreach easier, but loyalty will still be earned the old-fashioned way — through follow-through, transparency, and shared experience.

The Rise of Digital Noise — and How to Stand Out

We're already living in a time of digital overload. Everyone's in your inbox. Everyone's posting content. Everyone's networking at scale.

So how do you stand out?

You slow down. You show up. You do what others don't.

You follow up with a call instead of a link. You write a handwritten note. You remember the details. You invest real time where everyone else is phoning it in.

The future won't reward the loudest voice — it'll reward the most *authentic* one.

Hybrid Relationships Are the New Normal

Some of the deepest professional relationships I've built in recent years started online. That's just the world we live in now. But digital connection isn't the end goal — it's the starting point.

If you want to turn digital contacts into real allies, you've got to take it offline. Break bread. Shake hands. Look people in the eye. That's where trust is built. That's where ideas take root. That's where long-term partnerships are born.

The New Superpower: Knowing When to Lead and When to Listen

The leaders of tomorrow won't just be great communicators — they'll be great listeners. They'll know how to cut through the noise by asking the right questions. They'll connect not just with minds, but with motives.

AI can simulate a conversation. But it can't build a relationship. It can't see the moment when someone needs a word of encouragement. It can't sense when silence is more powerful than a pitch.

That's still your job.

What Doesn't Change

No matter how advanced the tools become, the fundamentals won't change:

- **People still want to be seen.**
- **They want to be heard.**
- **They want to work with people they trust.**

You can't outsource that.

So if you're thinking about the future of networking, don't just ask, "How do I scale?" Ask, **"How do I stay real while the world speeds up?"**

The answer isn't more tech. It's more trust.

And if you build your network on that foundation, I promise you — no matter what tools come along — you'll be ready.

7. What Comes Next

If you've read this far, you've probably figured it out: I've spent my life building.

I've built companies, led teams, launched technologies, and created opportunities — but more importantly, I've built trust. I've built relationships. I've built a network of people who show up, speak truth, and get things done.

That foundation led me into the world of politics, where I stepped forward to run for the U.S. Senate. And while I've since suspended that campaign, the mission didn't end — it simply evolved. I'm now serving as the **Executive Director of the Jerry Ambrose Veterans Council**, working every day to support those who've served our country, especially the veterans who too often fall through the cracks.

In this new chapter, I'm still knocking on doors. I'm still listening to small business owners, parents, farmers, and veterans who feel forgotten. I'm still building bridges — not for political gain, but for real people who need real solutions.

Leadership isn't about titles. It's about service. It's about accountability. It's about showing up — again and again — even when the spotlight fades.

So what's next?

More building. More listening. More leading from the front lines — this time, in the trenches of veteran advocacy, mental health support, and community transformation.

Because the network effect doesn't end in the boardroom — it grows stronger when it serves something greater than yourself.

Megan Watson was raised in Reno, NV and specializes in interior design, sales, and sales training. She has a passion for natural healing, holistic living and her three dogs, including one named after Dolly Parton.

When training individuals or a team, she focuses on the internal roots of personal development followed by strategy and implementation. The natural love she has for people is her greatest asset. Her nearly fifteen years of background in interior design has shaped how she sees beauty in all corners of her world. With her instinctive eye for beauty and assured sense of scale, her design is intentional, beautiful, and intimate. Megan's objective and passion always remain the same: to attain the highest level of achievement in producing memorable, highly defined interiors that deeply reflect the client's own personal history. Whether creating a peaceful home oasis or an intentional commercial office space that sparks creativity and injects energy into a room, she comes to genuinely love her clients and the projects that behold new journeys.

CHAPTER 18
Move Your Mountains

By Megan Watson

If you Want to Go Fast, Go Alone

If you Want to Go Far Go Together

-African Proverb

I welcome you with a smile and a sunflower heart. Thank you for being here. I don't have some big fancy story. I don't have a laundry list of accolades. I'm not some "guru." I am the gal still running for her dreams. My background is interior design and sales. I am a single mother and had my first of two daughters at 19. I have been on my own since I was 15 and took my GED before entering college, which I never completed. During my years of motherhood, I struggled financially. I was raised humbly by my mother and father, who divorced when I was five. My mother remarried when I was young to who would become an abusive stepfather. For context, you can associate me with a laundry list of "disadvantage tags" (teen mom, first-gen, low income, etc.). I refuse to allow these "tags" to define me. I say this because it doesn't matter as much where you came from as where you're going in this beautiful life we have been given. Networking is not reserved for the wealthy or the ones who seemingly have it all figured out and put together. We can create an incredible network regardless of our starting points.

I have always believed that the Lord has been a lamp to my path. He has placed angels in my life along the way who have not only guided me but supported me in the kindest, wisest, most loving ways that I can never pay back. When we seek answers from the most loving creator, we are bound to receive them. "If you think you're too small to make a difference, try sleeping with a mosquito." The Lord has a divine plan for your path. Our lives are shaped not only in His perfect timing but also among the living angels that we're destined to meet. He is my favorite treasured connection and relationship. We don't always feel that His timing is perfect. We feel pressure to meet life's needs, support the people we love, and to live for something greater than ourselves. This is our innate calling. I call it "the nudge." Lean in. Lean in to the nudge. You are worthy and, most importantly, called. I am sending you love and have prayed over the hearts who fall upon these words. If you're reading this, that is you.

You are reading this chapter merely because of the power of connection, the power of heart, and the power of listening to your gut and making a move. One by one, the "next move" becomes an ever-changing sum of many. They're like our own personal "Pangea", an arrangement of shifts in mindset, choices, habits, and "leaning into the nudge" that allows new formation. If you question your worth, your value, or your capability, I'm giving you permission to let go of that right now. Seriously. At the end of this paragraph, pause. Take a deep breath. One GREAT big one in. One GREAT big one out. Ten seconds each if you can. Then repeat, but this time I want you to do it while reflecting on what burns in your heart. What is the "nudge"? Ask yourself, "What is stopping me?" In the words of Marie Forleo, "Everything is Figureoutable." It is in the roadblocks that we find the path. Detours leave us with answers—"Detour here," "Go this way." In reality, detours become some of the best blessings that show up in our lives. Give yourself a pause. Let's breathe. Trust the process; stick with me. Take your first breath and imagine that you are breathing in the most important move you can make right now, feeling the feeling that you would feel in the moment when, in hindsight, you reflect and realize you are living in the fruit of those moves—the big ones, the little ones, the scariest and most exciting. Who did you need to become? Who did you need to meet? What does it feel like to become that person who has been yearning to come out, beckoning from the deepest places inside of you? Now close your eyes and breathe in. Breathe in, visualizing your next most important move. As you breathe out, breathe the doubt, the "roadblocks," the "detours," and anything else that feels heavy. Breathe out the boulders. Do this seven times. After your final deep breath in and out, add an eighth. Speak the words out loud: "I have permission, I am worthy, it is done."

My father was a caretaker. He cared for the horses, the pasture, and all the other needs that come with a vast property. I was raised in one of the most beautiful, wealthiest neighborhoods in our "Biggest Little City," despite living in poverty. I'm going to take you back into a fractional moment in my life when I was young… probably somewhere around the third or fourth grade. I sat at the kitchen table with my long brown hair that my dad had tightly plastered with hairspray into a ponytail that practically gave me a facelift every morning. My father, sister, and I lived in a one-bedroom condo that was built above the horse barn. Sitting at that kitchen tabletop my father had beautifully painted with a southwestern border (He was quite the artist). I was supposed to be getting my homework done. Instead, all I could find myself doing was staring out the kitchen window into the pasture watching the horses, the butterflies, and anything else that was more in line with my natural pleasures. It was always difficult for me to stay focused in school. I believe this is because without purpose, we find ourselves at a crossroad. It's an internal weight that turns feather weight to boulder weight. Ultimately, these bricks lead to some sort of conflict not only with ourselves but with others. We fail to meet expectations. My father walked into the condo after finishing up on the riding lawnmower. Sometimes he would let us sit on it with him while he cruised around in the sun, tending the grounds with care. I loved those moments with him and would much rather have been outside with him in the sun. He entered our home with frustration after finding me, again, not doing my homework. He was repeating himself for me to do something that really was pretty simple. This moment made me feel inadequate, like I had somehow failed my father, let him down, and upset him. I never really felt like I met his expectations and felt that I could rarely make him happy. I wasn't aware at that time that moments like this arrive to all of us in some way—all throughout our lives. We come to a point where that feeling of bricks and boulders arrives while attempting to execute normal routines. We focus on meeting external expectations. When we feel the bricks and the boulders, it's our internal compass speaking out, crying deep somewhere in the depths of our soul.

In life, we all face seasons of change. When we get sick, we seek medicine based on our symptoms and illness. We start to experience "symptoms" that make us feel uncomfortable, unhappy, and even sometimes trapped. During these times, it's impossible to not feel what I call "the nudge." When we are not in alignment with our natural calling, "symptoms" will often show up as constant doors being shut that were once opened. They also show up looking like every door we try to open becomes locked shut no matter how much we pray, beg, and barter with God to fulfill our requests. For whatever reason, no matter what we do, things don't quite feel right. This is redirection. Time is the truest antidote, and the only thing that brings answers.

We find answers in hindsight. Hindsight is some version of 20/20, varied by perspective. As we later reflect on our lives, we see how we were divinely protected or simply unwilling to allow a lesson that was right before our eyes that we could not or would not acknowledge. My mother always said, "The lesson repeats until learned." Sometimes the lesson hits us with a feather and sometimes, an anvil. Let's avoid playing Wile E. Coyote. Learn to listen to the feathers. Not only are the detours in our lives designed to help us, they are often there to bring us straight to surrender. Gabrielle Bernstein says, "When you think you've surrendered, surrender some more." Without these seemingly inconvenient times in our life, we would not ever find ourselves with the willingness to make the adjustments necessary to fulfill our purpose. None of us have just one. Once we achieve an important milestone on our journey of purpose, it seems that we again grow unsatisfied with the life before us that we had once prayed for. We are in constant evolution and constant discovery. So whether this chapter finds you on the mountaintop or deep in the valleys, perhaps with a ball and chain tied to your ankle in the middle of the Pacific Ocean, I promise your next favorite chapter is yet to be lived. I believe in you. Do the thing. In the words of Billy Joel—(insert piano music here) "When will you realize, Vienna waits for you."

AI is replacing lots of things right now, from marketing automation to manual labor jobs and countless revolutions that are yet to be. BUT there are still things only human souls can do. Things that only human hands can create and hearts can touch. From delicate, intricate artistry to meeting someone who connects soul deep, human souls were meant to create, to connect, to dig in the earth with our bare hands tending to our gardens. Today we are vastly missing out on the basic foundations that have formed humanity. We are all artisans. One thing that can never be replaced is the gift of the human soul. No algorithm can co-create soul to soul and achieve the same outcome. It is divine. Appointed. It's solid, and it's human. It's one of those rare things that will never be automated. It's a journey of destiny, as long as we choose that we want it and act. You can't outsource connection and you can't download soul. No machine can replace the magic of what happens when we create something with our hearts.

We have all heard "the American dream." What is your dream? You might have many. What is the most important one right now? "The (insert your name here) dream." Write it out daily. Who do you need to meet? What rooms do you need to step into? For me right now, my dream is to build my businesses so that I can plant permanent homes for foster children. That is a God-led dream. It was laid upon my heart and has never left. God gives us unique gifts that only we can contribute. Similar gifts delivered from someone else simply don't land the same. I remember one day in church, listening to our pastor's sermon. He asked a question to the congregation. "Who thinks they know their spiritual gifts? Raise your hand." Hands went up. Then he said, "If you don't think you understand your spiritual gifts, raise your hand." Many hands went up. His message was, "If you don't know what your spiritual gifts are, that's OK. God is allowing your circumstances and experiences to help." ... "And to those of you who raised your hand and believe you know what your spiritual gifts are, I challenge you to consider that there's a possibility you may be wrong." He was right. We unlock new levels of ourselves as life evolves and we begin to recognize pieces of ourselves that we could not have seen or known were inside of us. We all have dreams. We are also responsible for building them.

As we move through this beautiful life we have been given, what I have found is that when I begin to take the steps necessary,

God places the right humans in my path. Opportunities appear. Connection is the reason I have been blessed with the opportunity to share these words here on these pages. (Thanks Ken Walls!) Without question, every message, new connection, or lesson was meant for me at that particular time. Every single opportunity in my life has been the result of an introduction, and I also know that I've changed lives by making meaningful connections. Our connections, however, start at a young age. They are bred into us for the good and also the not-so-great. Later, life roars its ugly head when we face new seasons. We attract what we still need to heal. Finding mentorship and a good circle of humans comes with no shortage of getting bumped and bruised, but also has gifted me happiness and people that inspire me and that I trust. I've also learned that if life is bumping me around I might've had something to do with it. Discernment. I have paid for services that were never delivered and I have had betrayals I never expected, yet I have also found enjoyment and pleasure through the sorting. We sift through the rocky sands where we eventually find gems. Always be human over hustle; it attracts the ones worth keeping. As the saying goes, "People don't care how much you know until they know how much you care." Always lead with value.

Throughout all of the seasons of life, we are planted and planting. I love the imagery in Psalm 1. We are to be rooted. Without roots, trees would surely fall. Just like the trees, our appearance in the winter is never the same in spring, summer, and fall. During the winter, trees dig their roots deeper into the soil so that in the spring, their blooms may be beautiful and their growth evident. Never be afraid of bare branches. That is where the blossoms grow. How can we contribute without first understanding and planting our roots?

I can't think of any one particular person I have met that was the "most significant." My life has become more of a compilation than single moments of individuals. What I do know, however, is that I have put myself into uncomfortable rooms and spaces where I either became inspired by or had the opportunity to be introduced or mentored by some of the greatest humans I have ever known. I am highly introverted. When my daughters were little, I became very isolated and began to fear the world. I had been in a long-term abusive relationship with their father and ultimately couldn't even hear a knock at my front door without high levels of anxiety. I knew that I needed to force myself into uncomfortable situations in order to overcome that place in my life. I intentionally applied for a commissioned sales job because it forced me to connect with people to earn a living and to provide for myself and my children. We build the culmination of our lives one step of the journey at a time, not in one swift bold step.

Humans are interdependent. Just like a garden that needs the bees, the trees, and the mixture of plants that help each other thrive in the gardens, variety is the epitome of our entire universe. Removing just one thing could change the entire ecosystem of our lives. So can adding to it. Take for example Yellowstone, where the elk population exploded and wreaked havoc on the range. Yellowstone was in trouble. Wolves were returned in 1995 after being absent for 70 years due to hunting eradication. When the wolves were returned, the elk population declined, protecting the valleys from overgrazing. The wolves saved Yellowstone. The absence of just one creature deprived such a beautiful place of the beauty that once flourished. The world needs you. We all need each other. "Self-made"—who honestly can say this? I cringe when I hear or read this. Take a look around you right now where you are. If you're in nature, it is built with millions of tiny and large organisms. If you're in a building, think about how many people it took to construct just the floor below your feet. Materials had to be sourced, supply chains had to be in order, sales staff were involved, installers, inspectors, and even ongoing maintenance like cleaning and repair. We do NOTHING as a party of one. We can accomplish much with "we" and very little with "me." We can't sell anything without anyone to sell to. We can't fulfill our services without the work of others. We are interdependent, not independent. We were designed to be woven, not merely single strands of thread. What is fabric without the weaving? We are but strands of thread; we must be woven.

The most profound changes happen with smaller, consistent interactions over time. Joining an entrepreneur group landed me a free VIP ticket at Grant Cardone's 10X Growth Con event in Miami. While I was there, I found myself in the corporate VIP rooms talking to some of the best marketers, coaches, contractors, and salespeople in their industries. I also got to meet Sara Blakely. I don't get goo goo over people. I view humans as humans and consider them by their heart, not just their accomplishments. However, when I met Sara Blakely, I FORGOT MY NAME. She inspires me so much with her grit, intelligence, and perseverance that I actually forgot my name while introducing myself. Growing up, her dad used to encourage her and her brother to fail. At the dinner table, her father would ask them, "What did you fail at this week?" She said that if they didn't have something to tell him then he was actually disappointed. He high-fived her when she failed on her attempts. He celebrated her losses. What it did was condition her definition of failure—not defined by outcome, but by not trying. I remember her talking about when she was invited to be on Richard Branson's show *Rebel Billionaire*. She was cast as the girl who is afraid of heights and was going to make "really good TV." Instead, she faced her fear, set a world record, and proved that we don't know what we're capable of until we try. She found herself jumping off the Victoria Gorge in Africa with a bungee cord attached to her. There was a man on her team, dangling in the air by a crane 10 feet out from the cliff. Each person was required to jump off of the cliff without getting a running start. If the man caught you, you were okay, and they put you back on the cliff. If you missed, you fell 385 feet off the cliff from a bungee cord. She was the only one to accomplish this. When they asked her how she did it, she said that she was looking six feet above the man's head. That was her aim. Everyone else looked at his face before the jump and caught his feet. We might not hit what we aim for, but when we overshoot, we have a much better chance. The point here is that you are capable of a beautiful life your heart pines for. When I am working with clients on a project for their home, I use what I call "The Step Back approach." When they are undecided about a luxury item or a need that they are considering replacing or leaving out altogether, I ask them to imagine that their project is complete and they went without it. When we are able to bring hindsight into the present, our goals become more clear. There's nothing worse than looking back after making investments of time, resources and efforts to only later think, "If I would have just ____".

Make sure of a few things before you make your next moves. Get superb clarity, tying all of these efforts into a larger crystal-clear goal. Second, get clear on how bad you want your goal. We all wonder, when reality sits in, if it's worth it. It's easy to say yes to things that make our skin crawl, like writing a book, asking strangers for their business, or speaking in front of a room full of people when we're very clear on why we're doing it. It's always easy to make the decisions. It's not always easy to carry them out. We ask ourselves, *Is it worth it? Is it going to work?* Ask yourself, *If it didn't work the way I want, would it still be worth it?* The clarity of the fruit we seek gives us the roots to weather all the seasons of doubt that will undeniably come as we execute the requirements to "talk to that person," "move to that city," or whatever the path may be.

Now go back to paragraph one and breathe life into your dreams. You are only a few connections away. Lean into the nudge, move your mountains. I believe in you. You have permission.

Ken is a number one best-selling author, CEO of a marketing and Web development firm, and the creator of **LeadFlow360**, a comprehensive lead generation, marketing,g and sales tool for entrepreneurs and

sales professionals that is mobile and fully automated, doing the work so you don't have to. Visit https://www.leadflow360.pro.

He is also the creator of the **GrowLive Academy** and **Grow Live Inner Circle**, a comprehensive course and mastermind focused on helping people successfully use social media, video, and networking to build their personal or business brand and generate revenue. Visit https://www.growliveacademy.com.

Ken's passion is helping people succeed. Ken hosts a podcast called *Breakthrough Walls,* where he interviews celebrities and successful entrepreneurs who share their stories to help people overcome influences that may be holding them back. He also works one-on-one with clients who want to level up or experience their breakthrough.

Ken has written eight books; his first, *Breakthrough Walls: Turning Pain Into Profit,* is available on Amazon. Connect with Ken at https://www.kenwalls.com.

CHAPTER 19
The Network Effect

By Ken Walls

As I reflect on my life and the power that networking with other human beings has had on it, it is actually quite mind-boggling to me. I can promise you that every single success that I've experienced in life has in some way been a direct result of other people that I've networked with and become friends with. The flip side of that coin is that every time I've had a failure in my life or a massive setback, it's because I didn't network with the right people. Or I tried to go it alone.

When I was about seven or eight years old, I realized that if I wanted to have money, I needed to get out and meet the right people. That started with me pulling a lawn mower around the little town that I grew up in in Ohio. I went door-to-door, meeting people, asking them if I could mow their yards. Afterwards, I'd ask them if they knew any neighbors I could talk to, and who else they knew that needed their lawn mowed? It came to me as a very intuitive thing, even at that young age, fifty years ago.

In my early twenties, I started in a sales position with a company, and I quickly realized that if I wanted to make it and make it big, I was going to have to learn how to get referrals. In fact, I knew that referrals would be the lifeblood of my sales career. And it didn't matter to me if I made a big sale, an average sale, or a small sale. It truly didn't matter because I knew that everyone knows other people.

I was directly involved in developing door-to-door sales programs for the home security industry and the satellite dish industry back in both of their infancies. One of the most important parts of either of those programs was that, if you signed someone up, you found out who their neighbor was on both sides of their home (to the left and to the right), and found out who the two or three neighbors were across the street, because typically they would know them.

I have been blessed and fortunate enough to build massive companies doing multi-millions of dollars a year in business, primarily based on building referral networks. Back in 2002, I had a major life change; probably the biggest shift in my life I've ever had. And I found myself completely broken - financially, spiritually, emotionally, and in every other way. Again, I realized that I needed to meet people, but I knew that I had to have a filtration system to meet the right people. As I met the right people over the next couple of years, I started to build something really amazing. Through that referral network, I built my very first professional website for a Mercedes-Benz dealership. While at the grand opening of that Mercedes-Benz dealership, I was introduced to one of the most famous chefs in the world by the name of Chef Hartmut Handke. Chef Handke had a restaurant called Handke's Cuisine in Columbus, Ohio, and he needed a website. So I built his website, and I started building this amazing portfolio of very high-end clients that just continued to snowball and build and build. And here we are today, still creating websites, marketing programs, and web applications for people all over the world.

Fast forward to the year 2014, when I had just hired a brand new salesperson with no sales experience. I decided to look at some videos on YouTube, hoping to find a training system to help this young guy learn sales because I just didn't have the time to invest in training him every single day. That's when I came across some videos by a guy named Grant Cardone. I remember when I first watched his videos, I was like, "This guy is crazy." And I meant that in a good way. He was just really intense, so I reached out to his office, and they ended up closing me on spending $1,000/month for 36 months on their online sales training system.

I started watching Grant on live streams. I started hearing him say things like, "If you want to grow, you have to flow power to power." At first, I had no idea what he was talking about. But as I expanded my mind and really started listening, it all started to make sense to me. Grant would say things like, "Man, if you want to grow your business and you want to grow your life, you've got to help people who are already doing better than you. And I can remember thinking, "What in the world do I have to offer somebody that has a net worth of over a hundred million dollars?" But he kept saying, "Money follows attention, and I want everybody on planet earth to know who I am." And then I thought, "Okay, well, I don't have a huge reach on social media, but I have a big mouth, and I can tell everybody in the world about this guy and see if I can get on his radar." My target was to get on Grant Cardone's radar. It didn't take long, only a matter of a few months. I started live streaming. I started talking about Grant and all of his programs, and I definitely got on his radar. In fact, I won a trip on his private jet as a result of promoting him so much. That trip turned into me going to his office in Miami, Florida, and sitting with him for three hours, with him coaching me one-on-one. It absolutely changed my life.

I ended up having a show on Grant Cardone TV for a few months. And I was becoming known all over the world because of the millions of followers he had. He would give me a shout-out all the time. Grant and I did live streams together and built a friendship from a distance. Because of that investment I made in my new sales guy and everyone else in my company, I really started to flourish in every way. I began meeting other people who are very well known and have celebrity status. I started building relationships with people again, all over the world, who were doing better than me financially in their businesses. I flowed power upwards. I flowed power to people who were in power, and it helped me so much. It really helped me grow significantly.

When I started doing my own live streams back in 2014, I had never done anything like that before. I was absolutely petrified to do it, but I did it anyway. And I did it a lot. When I first started, I was livestreaming in 10-15 minute segments, probably five to ten times a day on average. In the first year, I did well over 800 live streams. Since then, I've now done more than 4000 live streams. I have since founded and lead the GrOwLive Academy, where I teach people live streaming and podcasting. I have students all over the world.

A little more than seven years ago, I started my own podcast called *Breakthrough Walls*, and it's currently ranked in the top 10% of all podcasts in the world. Seven years ago, I was at a crossroads again in my business and in my life, and I decided that a much faster way to build my network would be to start interviewing other people, celebrities, and entrepreneurs who already have huge networks. I thought, "If I interview them and let them come on and share their life story, and I share that with my audience, they're going to share it as well with their audience, and their audience has no idea who I am, so they would slowly start getting to know me." And that's exactly what happened! I have now interviewed more than 650 celebrities and entrepreneurs who have come onto my show and shared their life stories, wisdom, and knowledge. Many of the amazing people I've had on my show, I have built friendships and relationships with. I've helped many of them with marketing and websites and all kinds of fun things to help them grow their brands and businesses.

I would say one of the most important and valuable relationships that I've built over the last six years is with my best friend, Glenn Morshower. Glenn is a very famous actor who's been an actor for more than 50 years and has more than 280 credits on IMDb. But that's not what makes him special to me. What makes this guy special is his heart, intelligence, and desire to flood the world with inspiration and motivation to make each and every one of their lives better. Every person that Glenn comes in contact with walks away a better person. It's true for me, and I have witnessed it with thousands of other people as well. This friendship started because of my friendship with Bob Donnell, God rest his soul, and my buddy Joe Ingram. Starting a show and a podcast and opening up the ability for people to come on to my show and tell their life story has been one of the greatest things that I've ever done. It's been absolutely amazing.

This book exists because I decided I wanted to write a book about networking, and I wanted to include a lot of amazing people. Every single person who has written a chapter in this book is a direct result of my networking and having a large podcast. And I don't say that to brag. I tell you that so that you can feel it in your heart and know that if I am capable of building something like this, then so are you and so is anyone else.

If you could look at my cell phone call history on a day-to-day basis, you would be amazed at the number of people I talk to who have made and continue to make a positive impact on this world. Just yesterday, I spoke with my dear friend Mark Victor

Hansen. Mark is the co-creator of the *Chicken Soup for the Soul* book series and brand, and we talked for quite a while. I still have the voicemail saved from when Mark first reached out to me because he wanted to be on my show. He was referred to me by Bob Donnell. Bob passed away recently, but he was one of the most masterful networkers, giving, caring, and loving human beings that I've ever known.

One of the most amazing things that happened to me involves Mark. He was having his biography written by Mitzi Perdue of the Perdue chicken family. He called me and said, "I would love it if you would let Mitzi interview you for my biography to tell the story about when we met." At first, I thought he was joking, and I said, "Okay, sure." If I'm completely honest, I did not expect it to happen. But it did, and in Mark Victor Hansen's biography titled *Relentless,* there is a whole chapter in his book about me and the power of storytelling. It's chapter 27. And yes, I will always remember that.

I have also written books with the legendary King of Sales, Jeffrey Gitomer, Dr. Bernie Siegel, and with all the amazing people in this book. Everything that has occurred is 100% a direct result of the networking I've done and the energy and effort I've put into building that network and giving back to the people in that network. I would say that the biggest factor in building the network of amazing people in my life is a direct result of my desire to help other people. When I meet somebody new, my mind automatically goes to a place of trying to figure out how I can help them connect with people, products, or services that will help them expand what they are doing. We've all met the people who you can immediately tell are only interested in what's in it for them. Those are called takers. There's an old saying that goes "givers have to set boundaries" because takers rarely do.

My buddy Glenn has a saying that goes like this: "Today I live in such a way that tomorrow I'm proud of my yesterday." If you really want to build a beautiful life with a massive network of people who can help you, who want to help you, and who will help you, then you have to start by giving, not taking. You have to start with the energy of "how can I help this other person?" You have to start with the energy of "who can I connect them with to help them," and do not expect anything in return. Just stay aware and alert, and overdeliver on helping them.

When I first met Mark Victor Hansen and his wife, I was incredibly nervous because he is the number-one best-selling author of all time. But beyond that, I developed a friendship with them immediately. I felt the deep desire to help them with their new book and get them in front of as many people as I possibly could who also do podcasts and shows, to help them rocket their book to the top. And that is exactly what happened.

The same thing goes for my friendship with Glenn Morshower. Glenn and I met literally within days of the shutdown during the COVID pandemic. My desire was to help him solve a problem that he was having with his acting school because he could no longer conduct classes in person. So, I helped him by showing him what was possible online using Zoom. Now, he's taken that to a completely different level and has more students in his acting class than he ever had with students all over the world joining on Zoom; it's pretty amazing.

It's quite the honor to say that I'm friends with all three of Zig Ziglar's children as well. And I told Tom Ziglar when I had him on my show that his father's number one quote for me is "You can have everything in life that you want if you'll just help enough other people get what they want in life."

It is my hope and dream that millions of people around the world read this book and absorb this material, applying all of the lessons to their own lives and to the lives of the people they are networking with.

I hope you take every word of this book, every lesson from every person in this book, and apply what's right for you in your life. I hope that if you don't already have it, you develop the desire to help other people get what they want out of life, so you can also experience the truth behind Zig Ziglar's words: "You will have everything you want in life and so much more."

God bless you and your family. I pray that you just go out and help other people.

www.ingramcontent.com/pod-product-compliance
Lightning Source LLC
Chambersburg PA
CBHW070920120626
46546CB00001B/336